SONG STARTERS

365 Lyric, Melody, & Chord Ideas to Kickstart Your Songwriting

by

Robin Frederick

SOUND EXPERIENCE BOOKS

Los Angeles, CA

Song Starters: 365 Lyric, Melody & Chord Ideas to Kickstart Your Songwriting.

Cover Design by Panagiotis Lampridis
Author Photo by Gil Cope
Page Design by Lynn King for Nosy Rosy Designs
Text Editing by Bethany Rubin

ISBN-13: 978-0-9654789-3-9

» Acknowledgements

Throughout this book, I've relied on hit songs to provide examples of song-writing techniques. In each case, I've given the name of the artist or band who recorded the song rather than the songwriter or songwriters. In some cases, the artist and songwriter are the same person. (I am always amazed by anyone with that many talents.) In other cases, the songwriter is the wizard behind the curtain who writes words and melodies so heartfelt and universal that any artist can sing them as if they are their own.

I urge you to take the time to research these songwriters yourself. Make it part of your writing routine. These writers are your mentors, offering creative solutions to problems and insights into the songwriter's craft with every song they write.

To track down the names of these sometimes elusive gurus, visit the online searchable databases at ASCAP (ACE Repertory) and BMI (BMI Repertoire). You can search by song title or recording artist. If you can't find the song there, search the internet using the song's title followed by the artist's name and the word "songwriter."

Once you know who these songwriters are, learn something about their writing process. Interviews are a great place to start. Check out song-writing, recording, and music industry magazines. An internet search will often turn up an interview in an online magazine, on YouTube, or on a songwriting website. (See "Learn More: Songwriters Tell All" at the end of this book for more search ideas.)

Over the years I've been writing and working in the music industry, I've learned that nothing gets creativity flowing like new ideas and information. When you learn something new, the best you can be gets better. So with this book, I'd like to offer a big "thank you" to all my teachers. I hope they will become yours, too.

Every song begins with one small idea,
one little leaf, then another and another.
Together they grow into a beautiful,
living expression of your heart and humanity.

—Robin Frederick

More books by Robin Frederick

Shortcuts to Hit Songwriting

Shortcuts to Songwriting for Film & TV

*Study the Hits: Learn the Secrets of Today's
Chart-Topping Hit Songs*

The 30-Minute Songwriter

Robin's books are available at Amazon.com and other retail book outlets.

Visit RobinFrederick.com to join Robin's songwriting email list.

» Contents

» HOW TO BEAT THE BLANK PAGE

First, there's a blank page. And there's you.

Ever since a prehistoric cave painter stared at a smooth wall of rock and wondered what to put on it, artists have been moaning about how intimidating it is to get started. Whether it's a white canvas, a clean sheet of typing paper, or a fresh computer screen, that first step is the hardest.

Of course, you can wait for inspiration, but those big "light bulb" moments tend to turn up at awkward times (the middle of the night, driving on the freeway) or they just don't show up at all. They're particularly reluctant to appear when you beg them to.

Blank page: one. You: zero.

Yes, you can sit down on your couch, guitar in hand, have a firm talk with your brain and force it to spit out something. That sometimes works. But more often, the "something" it spits out turns out to be nothing after all.

Blank page: two. You: zero.

Or you can do some outrageously creative exploring. Promise you won't keep any of it. Get playful. Take risks. Tell yourself you're just warming up. Listen to somebody else's music. Nothing serious going on here. Nooooo. No need to pay any attention to the songwriter on the couch. A few minutes of that and — aha! — suddenly you've got one! The germ of an idea. It's small, but you see where it can go. And next thing you know you're galloping after it.

The blank page is defeated! You win!

When songwriting becomes too serious and your Inner Critic goes into overdrive, just imagine you're a toddler in a room full of toys. A child will start playing with one thing, drop it, and go on to something new without a second thought. Then maybe come back to the first thing, use it in some crazy way, or throw in a third thing. It's all about exploring, creating, playing, and enjoying.

I'm not saying you don't have to work hard at crafting a song, but that comes later in the process. Starting a song should be more like *play* than *work.* If we take ourselves too seriously too soon, the joy and the creativity go out of it.

I wrote this book so we can stop taking ourselves so seriously. Start writing songs with a child's eagerness and playfulness. Stop being afraid of that blank cave wall and finally paint a darn bison on it. So, whenever you're ready, let's get this songwriting thing rolling!

Robin Frederick
October, 2016
Los Angeles, California

» GET THE MOST FROM SONG STARTERS

There are thousands of ways to start a song because there are as many ways to start as there are songwriters. But sometimes when we sit down to write, we just can't think of any. That's when a Song Starter can be your best friend.

Song Starters are situations, titles, characters, melody patterns, rhythm grooves, and chord progressions that help you get your ideas flowing. Because everyone's creative comfort zone is different, there's no single way to work with Song Starters that's better than another. Here are a few suggestions:

- You can focus on one type of Song Starter — Lyrics, Melody, Chords, or Music Tracks — and explore it.

- You can jump around the book, trying anything that sounds interesting.

- You can use or reuse several Starters in one day.

- You can use a different Starter each day for a year. There are 365, so you'll be fine except for leap years. (Take a vacation day and go crazy.)

ESSENTIAL TIPS FOR USING SONG STARTERS

1. <u>RECORD YOUR WORK AS YOU GO.</u> It's easy to forget a good idea when a lot of material is coming fast, so keep a recorder nearby. You can use a computer, digital voice recorder, smartphone, or cassette recorder; whatever is close by and easy to use. Of course, good ol' pencil and

paper is handy, too. But if a lyric arrives with a melody or beat, get it down on the recorder.

Don't be too quick to turn down an idea. If you think there's a chance it could turn into something, record it. A lyric or melody line that sounds ho-hum when you first think of it may seem absolutely inspired when you come back later and listen with fresh ears.

2. <u>CREATE A SONG IDEA LIBRARY.</u> Working with Song Starters can unleash a torrent of new material. Once you get used to doing it, it's pretty easy to write down or record an idea. It can be much harder to look up that idea later on when you want to use it in a song. Bringing some organization to these brilliant flashes of inspiration can help you turn them into finished songs or provide you with a wonderful pre-chorus, bridge, or verse when you need one.

- **Organize your music and lyric ideas by *mood*.** The single, most important element shared by both the music and lyrics of a song is the emotional tone. A quirky, feel-good lyric works best with a quirky, feel-good melody and rhythm. Make a list of emotions and moods that broadly describe the types of songs you want to write. Here are four important, basic categories to get you started.

  1. Happy, joyful, upbeat, hopeful

  2. Sad, depressed, despairing

  3. Quirky, fun, surprising, whimsical

  4. Angry, aggressive, rebellious

- **Descriptive titles help.** Give each of your ideas a title that suggests the emotional feel of the music or lyric, and then add it to your list of emotions and moods in the appropriate place. When you want to find an upbeat lyric that might work with a whimsical melody, you'll know where to start looking for one.

- **Dedicate a short session each week to organizing.** Nothing kills a creative buzz faster than worrying about where you're going to file stuff. So, keep your organizing time separate from your creative time. Set aside an hour each week to go through your latest ideas and add them to your moods list. Make sure the titles suggest the emotional tone and that they're sorted correctly.

- **Use organization to boost your creative output.** Every couple of months, revisit some of the files in your idea library. Listen to the recordings and read the lyrics. Then pull out a few you'd like to work on. Don't let ideas gather dust for too long without giving them a little TLC. If you find you're hanging onto something without working on it, use some of the Song Starters in this book to get it going.

3. <u>TAKE ALL THE IDEAS YOU CAN GET.</u> If you're hauling in melody ideas like fish in a feeding frenzy, go ahead and stash away as many as you can. Don't stop to worry if you'll ever write another lyric. Don't fret if your recording sounds ragged. Just take all the melody ideas you can get. Opportunities like these are priceless.

The same holds true when lyric ideas are swarming but melodies are nowhere to be found. Keep your lyric ideas in a notebook or text file. If they come with rhythmic phrasing, record them. Don't stop to think about song structure. Don't wonder if you're writing a hit song or not. Just get it all down. Later on you can sort, toss out, keep, rewrite, and do what's needed. But when inspiration is being generous, take whatever it gives you.

Once you've gathered up a store of melodies, use the Lyric Starters section of the book to help you develop your song further. If you've got a bunch of lyric ideas, use the Melody Starters section to help you complete verses and choruses.

4. <u>KEEP ALL OF YOUR MAJOR DRAFTS.</u> Storage is cheap. Flash drives, external hard drives, DVDs and — if you're old school — paper, cassettes, and tape recorders are so inexpensive there's really no excuse for losing a version of your song that might be THE ONE. If you decide to make substantial changes to a recorded version of a song idea, keep a backup of the file or recording in case you decide to come back to it. I love the idea of the UNDO button. Anything you do, you can undo if you keep your earlier version.

5. <u>USE SONG STARTERS TO WARM UP.</u> Song Starters can help you loosen up before a serious writing session. Use them on your own or with co-writers. Choose one and dash off something quickly. Toss it and move on to another idea. Toss that one. Write another. Don't worry about how good it is. It's just a warm up, a practice session. If you wind up liking something, keep it. If not, dump it all in the trash. This is a great way to fool your Inner Critic into looking the other way while your creativity takes a lap around the track.

6. <u>BE THE CREATIVE, ORIGINAL WRITER YOU ARE.</u> The ideas, lyric phrases, melody patterns, and chord progressions in this book are yours to use. Change them or use them as is. Experiment and explore. Add or subtract words and notes. Try things backwards and forwards. Play with all of it. Give your inspiration a nudge — well, frankly, give it a shove — by exploring all of it, seeing the potential, getting your voice and toe-tapping feet going. Your creativity will light up when it sees the party getting started.

The lyrics and melodies of the hit songs referenced here are copyrighted, of course. I'll point out general songwriting tools and techniques you can learn from them and use in your own songs. Just be careful not to use any unique lyric, melody, or instrumental lines from those songs. But everything else... GO FOR IT!

PART ONE

SONG STARTERS: LYRICS

Use these Song Starters to rough out lyric ideas and create raw material you can build on. Make lists of short phrases — ten words or less — that capture any emotions, images, physical sensations, examples, or memories the Song Starter brings up for you. (Short phrases can be turned into lyric lines more easily than long paragraphs.)

Don't worry about rhyming for now. Avoid bending a line out of shape or changing the meaning to make it rhyme. It's more important to say what you want to say. Of course, if a rhyme happens to come along, by all means keep it.

The most effective lyrics communicate thoughts and feelings in a way listeners can feel, understand, and identify with. Keep your audience in mind while you write. Share your experiences and emotions in vivid pictures and memorable examples.

» START WITH A SITUATION

Starting your song with a situation can give you a lot to write about. It can provide passion, conflict, warmth, tragedy, or humor — depending on the people involved and the circumstances. What's going on in this situation? What is the singer feeling right now and why? Is there someone else involved? What are they saying or doing? Listeners love to be a fly on the wall, eavesdropping on someone else's life. Give them a good look.

PEAK MOMENTS: Every situation has a peak moment, a point where emotions run high, events come to a head, what was unclear comes into focus, or a decision is made. Look for this moment in each situation and build your song around it. A peak moment can make your song compelling, give it a sense of urgency, and bring it to life for listeners.

RELATIONSHIP SITUATIONS

1

Choose one of these two situations. Imagine it's happening to you. How does it feel? What do you see and hear? Write about it as if it's happening right now. Choose one or more of your lines to start your song.

- I just met you and I'm falling in love.
- People are trying to keep us apart.

2

Choose one of these two situations and describe what's happening as if you're telling a stranger about it. Keep them interested. Make them want to listen to you.

- I had a love I thought would last.

- I'm looking for someone special.

3

Find the peak moment in one of these two situations. What does the singer realize in that moment? What determines his or her next action? Start your song there.

- I think the excitement is going out of our relationship.

- I wonder if you're leaving me.

4

Choose one of these situations to write about. Answer the questions: Why did you choose that situation? What attracted you to it? Why is it important? No superficial answers now. Write down your thoughts and use them to start your song.

- I'm not ready to make a commitment.

- I found the love I've been searching for.

- Anything can happen if you let it.

- There are so many reasons to let go.

5

Choose one of these relationship situations and decide what the singer's role will be. Then ask yourself what the other person is feeling. Write one verse from the singer's point of view, then another verse from the other character's point of view. *(Example: "Somebody That I Used to Know" – Gotye)*

- It's too complicated to explain.

- I want you to trust me.

- I remember the first time I met you.

6

Imagine you're writing a screenplay. Select one of these situations and write the lines a character might say to justify an action they're about to take. Then turn those lines into a lyric.

- I'm leaving you. I've had it!

- Let me take you away from all this.

- Show a little respect!

- Frankly, my dear, I don't give a damn.

7

Choose one of these situations and finish the phrase: "What I really need to tell you is…" Use that line to start a verse or chorus.

- Two people at the altar getting married.

- Two people saying goodbye at an airport.

- Two people on a beach at sunset.

8

Choose one of these two situations. Imagine the other person in the song saying, "I don't understand. What do you mean?" Find different ways to explain yourself using images, examples, actions, or whatever it takes. Keep answering until you run out of ways to say what you mean. Use your answers in your lyric.

- I want you to love me like I love you.

- You make me feel like a million bucks.

9

Listen to any song on the list below. Look for the one line in the lyric that you feel expresses the situation best. Where is it located in the song? Write one or more original lines that could work in that spot instead. Use those lines to start a song of your own.

- "Apologize" – OneRepublic

- "I Heard It Through The Grapevine" – Marvin Gaye

- "I Think I Loved You Before I Met You" – Savage Garden

10

Choose one of the songs on this list. Listen to it and write down the situation in one sentence. How does the singer feel about it? How did the lyric describe that feeling? What kinds of words, images, and actions were used? Write a few lyric lines of your own that could replace some of the lines in the song. Write an original melody to go with them and add chords.

- "Halo" – Beyoncé

- "All Of Me" – John Legend

- "Let Her Go" – Passenger

11

Pick one of the songs on this list and listen to the lyric. Using the same situation, change the perspective. Write a few lines from the point of view of the person the singer is singing to. What is *their* situation? How are they handling what the singer is feeling and saying? Write a song they might sing in reply.

- "Say Something" – A Great Big World

- "Wind Beneath My Wings" – Bette Midler

- "Someone Like You" – Adele

CHALLENGES, SELF-DISCOVERY, AND LIFE SITUATIONS

12

Find the peak moment in one of these two situations, the moment in which the singer comes to a decision or realization. What does the singer realize? What does he or she decide to do about it? Build your lyric around that idea.

- I think I'm ready to reach for my dream.

- When will I stop pretending? When can I be who I really am?

13

Imagine yourself in one of these two situations. What would make you say a line like this? What's happening to you? Write down a list of phrases, images, and examples so that listeners can see what you see and feel what you feel. Build your song around those.

- Success is just around the corner. I can feel it!

- Nothing can keep me down. I'm a fighter!

14

Here are four situations that are common in today's teen and 'tween songs in the Pop genre. These listeners are very sensitive to songs that talk down to them or try to tell them how they ought to behave. Respect the difficulties they face. Put yourself in their shoes and write a song from their perspective.

- Growing up is hard, but there are good things about it, too.

- No one understands me. I feel isolated and alone.

- Being a kid these days is confusing. I get overwhelmed.

- I'm discovering who I am.

15

The following situations are common in the Country genre. Keep in mind that today's Country hits demand a fresh, honest look at these themes. Project yourself into the character and the life of the singer. Identify with it. Find parallels in your own life. Paint a vivid picture of the details of everyday life. What's important to the singer and why? Make lists of images, actions, and examples. Build your lyric around those.

- A job and a family are all I need to be happy.

- I've been kicked around, but I'll survive.

- Life's been good to me. I'm grateful.

16

Choose a situation from the list below and write about it as if you were talking to a stranger. These are generic sayings that everyone uses. Your challenge is to keep the listener interested. Put yourself in the situation and come up with fresh ways to express it, or imagine the questions a stranger would have and answer them in your lyric in unexpected ways.

- When life hands me a lemon, I make lemonade.

- I've learned that there's no time like the present.

- Actions speak louder than words. I do it; I don't just talk about it.

17

Listen to these songs and notice how each one describes a sense of hard-won freedom and independence. Describe a similar situation in your own words, as if you are personally experiencing it. What can you compare it to? What images and actions does it bring to mind? How does it make you feel physically and emotionally? Make a list of ideas and write a song on this theme.

- "Stronger (What Doesn't Kill You)" – Kelly Clarkson
- "Fight Song" – Rachel Platten
- "Roar" – Katy Perry

18

Listen to one of these two songs and describe the situation in your own words. Use short phrases (6 to 12 words) that can be turned into a lyric. Start a song with your own lines.

- "The Greatest Love" – Whitney Houston
- "Unwritten" – Natasha Bedingfield

19

Choose one of these songs and look for a line that sums up the singer's feelings about the situation. Write one or more original lines that the singer could have sung instead of that one. Find other ways to say it, or even a different angle on it. Use those lines to start a song of your own.

- "9 To 5" – Dolly Parton

- "The Promised Land" – Bruce Springsteen

- "Hard Workin' Man" – Brooks & Dunn

CELEBRATIONS, GOOD TIMES, AND PARTY SITUATIONS

20

Imagine yourself in one of these three situations. What do you feel? What are you doing? What do you see around you? What are other people feeling in that situation? Use the answers to those questions to start a song.

- I'm going out tonight and I just know I'll have the best time ever!

- My friends know how to party. We rock!

- It's your birthday. Let's celebrate!

21

Picture yourself in a situation where you might say one of the following phrases. Then imagine a stranger walks up to you asks: What do you mean? Why are you saying that? What does that feel like? (By the way, the stranger is your listener.) Use images, physical sensations, comparisons, and examples to show the listener what you mean.

- Everything is going my way.

- I'm living the good life.

- It feels great to kick back and relax.

22

Listen to one of these songs and look for a lyric line that sums up the singer's feelings. Write one or more original lines the singer could have sung instead of that one. Use those lines to start a song of your own.

- "I Gotta Feeling" – The Black Eyed Peas
- "Celebrate" – Kool and the Gang
- "Brand New" – Ben Rector
- "June: Good Days Start Here" – Tim Myers

23

Each of these songs features a location where people are having a good time. Choose one of these locations, or come up with one of your own and write a song expressing the good times people are having. Make your listeners feel as if they are there.

- "Groovin'" – The Young Rascals
- "Saturday In The Park" – Chicago
- "Dancing In The Street" – Martha and the Vandellas
- "Surfin' Safari" – The Beach Boys

24

Make a list of words, phrases, images, feelings, and activities you associate with good times, vacation, relaxing, summertime, partying, or just hanging out with friends. Then make a list of contrasting words and phrases, things you associate with hard work, stress, and tension. Write a lyric that uses words from both lists. This song is a great example.

- "It's Five O'clock Somewhere" – Alan Jackson and Jimmy Buffett

25

Listen to one of these songs and replace their chorus lyric with a lyric of your own, one that expresses a similar feeling. Create a new melody and chords for your lyric. Then, do the same with the verse.

- "Happy" – Pharrell Williams

- "The Best Day Of My Life" – American Authors

- "Summer Breeze" – Seals & Crofts

SOCIETY AND COMMUNITY SITUATIONS

26

Putting a human face on a social problem or giving a specific example of an injustice is an effective way to make people see things the way you do. Choose one of these situations and finish the phrase: "Here's a specific example of what I mean..." Use that line to start a verse. In your chorus, describe the emotion expressed by your example.

- I see an injustice and it makes me angry.

- I want to change things for the better.

27

Choose a situation from this list or use one of your own. Write it down. Imagine it. Now answer the question: Why did you choose that situation? What have you seen or what have you done that makes you feel it's important? Use your answer to start your song.

- Working together we can solve a problem.

- One person can make a difference.

- Our differences are on the outside. Inside we're all the same.

28

Find the peak moment in one of the situations in the list below, the moment in which the singer comes to a decision or a realization. What does the singer realize? What does he or she decide to do about it? Build your lyric around that idea.

- I'm discovering reasons to love my country/city/small town.

- I wonder if we can make a better tomorrow.

- I'm starting to understand that our children are the future.

29

Think of an image or action that you want people to take. Build your song around it. Listen to these songs for ideas.

- "Imagine" – John Lennon

- "Another Day In Paradise" – Phil Collins

30

Make a list of words, phrases, images, feelings, and activities you associate with the social issue or event you want to write about. Then make a list of contrasting words and phrases you associate with injustice, pain, or difficulties. Write a lyric that uses words from both lists. *(Example: "We Are the World" – U.S.A. For Africa)*

31

Give a cause or movement a human face by showing the effect it has on individual people. Listen to these songs for some ideas on how to do that, and then try it in a song of your own.

- "For What It's Worth" – Buffalo Springfield

- "Little Man" – Alan Jackson

- "A Change Is Gonna Come" – Sam Cooke

32

Write a song about the place where you live, or a place you remember. Paint a vivid picture by including details that make the listener see and feel what it's like to live there.

- "Tattoos On This Town" – Jason Aldean

- "Living For The City" – Stevie Wonder

- "Small Town" – John Mellencamp

- "Factory" – Bruce Springsteen

» START WITH A MEMORY

A strong memory is a good place to start a lyric. Vivid memories often have an emotional component which means they can be turned into memorable songs. When working with a memory, focus on the feelings that come along with it. You don't need to go into specifics like dates and names. Ask yourself why you remember this particular event or person. What kind of impact did this person or place have on you? Why was it important enough to store in your memory? Why do you think other people might like to hear about it?

Family photos, high school yearbooks, and scrapbooks can be a big help in recalling important events and people. Keep the image in front of you while you write to add energy and credibility to your song. If you don't have photos, use your imagination. Recreate the person or event as vividly as you can and relive the feelings you felt then.

WRITING SONGS FROM RECOLLECTIONS

33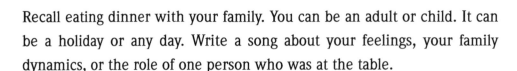

Recall eating dinner with your family. You can be an adult or child. It can be a holiday or any day. Write a song about your feelings, your family dynamics, or the role of one person who was at the table.

34

Remember a house where you used to live. In your memory, go from room to room recalling things that happened there. Choose one or more recollections and write about them. *(Example: "The House That Built Me" – Miranda Lambert)*

35

When you were a child, what did you want to be when you grew up? How does that compare with your life now? What did you actually end up doing? What would you like to tell your child-self about that? Start your chorus with the most important thing you'd like to say.

36

What was your favorite book or story when you were young? Why was it your favorite? Are there any parallels with your life now? Use that idea to start your lyric.

37

Remember a trip you took with your family. Make a list of things you recall about that trip. Why did those particular things stick in your memory? Was there an emotion or a person that made them more important? Write a song about the trip, focusing on the emotional or personal connection that made it stay with you.

38

Remember a past girlfriend or boyfriend. What happened to that relationship? What would you like to tell them now?
(Example: "Someone Like You" – Adele.)

39

Choose one of the songs on this list, one that comes close to an experience you've had. Write one or two lyric lines of your own that could replace lines in the song. Use those lines to start a new song.

Examples:

- "The Way We Were" – Barbra Streisand

- "I Did With You" – Lady Antebellum

- "Dear Marie" – John Mayer

- "Who Knew" – P!nk

40

Remember your life at specific ages or time periods and choose one to write about. Or treat your lyric as a short autobiography made up of snapshots from different times in your life.

Examples:

- "It Was a Very Good Year" – Frank Sinatra

- "Remember When" – Alan Jackson

- "7 Years" – Lukas Graham

- "Dirt Road Diary" – Luke Bryan

- "Coat Of Many Colors" – Dolly Parton

41

Think about a childhood or teenage friend. Is there anything you'd like to tell that person? What was left unsaid? Tell them in your lyric. *(Example: "Hello" – Adele)*

WRITING SONGS FROM PHOTOGRAPHS

42

While looking at a picture of your family, describe your feelings about the place, the occasion, or someone in the picture. Describe what was happening when the picture was taken, or create a situation around it. In your song, try talking to someone in the picture as if they are with you now.

Examples:

- "We Are Family" – Sister Sledge

- "Loves Me Like A Rock" – Paul Simon

- "Because Of You" – Kelly Clarkson

43

Look at a picture of yourself when you were younger and think about who you were, what you wanted, hoped for, loved, or feared. Write a song that expresses those feelings.

Examples:

- "Once When I Was Little" – James Morrison

- "At Seventeen" – Janis Ian

- "Fireflies" – Faith Hill

44

While looking at a picture of yourself as a child, write down what you would like to tell your child-self about life.

Examples:

- "Forever Young" – Bob Dylan

- "Back When I Knew It All" – Montgomery Gentry

45

Choose a holiday picture of your family. What's happening in the picture? What did this holiday look like, smell like, sound like, or taste like? Is there anything about this holiday in particular that stands out for you?

Examples:

- "White Christmas" – Bing Crosby

- "Wintersong" – Sarah McLachlan
- "Something About December" – Christina Perri

46

Look at a picture of a summer vacation. Maybe you're hanging out with high school friends or camping with your family. How do you feel when you think about it? Is there anything you learned from it that you use in your life today? Put your thoughts and feelings into a song.

Examples:

- "Summer Of '69" – Bryan Adams
- "Boys Of Summer" – Don Henley

47

Look through your high school or college yearbook and find a picture of someone you knew. What do you remember about that person and why? Write a song about what happened and who they might be now.

Examples:

- "Glory Days" – Bruce Springsteen
- "Photograph" – Nickelback
- "Crocodile Rock" – Elton John

48

All of the following songs use memories in one way or another. Listen to one or more of them and notice the role that memories play in the song lyric. Use that concept to start a song of your own.

- "In My Life" – The Beatles
- "We're Going To Be Friends" – The White Stripes
- "Photograph" – Ed Sheeran
- "When We Were Young" – Lucy Schwartz
- "Didn't We Almost Have It All" – Whitney Houston

WRITING SONGS FROM A SCRAPBOOK

49

Choose an item in a scrapbook. Why did you keep this item? What's the story behind it? What emotional significance does it have for you? Start your verse lyric by describing the item. In the chorus, tell listeners about the emotions it brings up for you.

50

Select an item in a scrapbook from an event or experience you shared with someone else. What was the importance of the event? Who did you share it with? Is that person still part of your life? Answer those questions and any others you think listeners might have. Remember, it's not the specific details of what happened but the feelings and emotional significance of those events that is important.

51

What's missing from your scrapbook? What do you wish you had that you don't? Why isn't it there? Imagine a blank space in the book. How would you feel if you could fill it with the missing item? Write a song about that feeling and answer some of the questions.

52

If you don't have a scrapbook, imagine one. What would you fill it with? What would you have to do to get hold of those items? How hard would it be? Answer these questions in your verse lyrics. In the chorus, tell the listener how you would feel about having those items, or how it feels not to have them.

» START WITH A CHARACTER

The world's best-loved books and movies feature strong, memorable characters. Just think of James Dean in *Rebel Without a Cause,* Marilyn Monroe in *Gentlemen Prefer Blondes,* Jamie Foxx in *Ray,* or Marlon Brando in *On The Waterfront.* We may not remember the plot, but we can easily recall these famous characters and even repeat some of their best lines.

In a song, you don't have a lot of time to tell listeners about your character. That's why you need to give them examples of how this character acts, talks, walks, and the physical details that will make your audience feel that they know this person as well as you do.

You can write your song as if singing to the character ("I'm talkin' to you…") or describe the character from a distance ("Let me tell you about him/ her…"). You can even be the character yourself ("I'm like this…"). You can also choose whether you want your listeners to feel sympathy for your character or dislike them. It's up to you. How do *you* feel about the character?

53

Choose one of these characters and give some examples of things they do that express who they are. Use one to start a verse.

- A rebel

- A shy wallflower

- A compulsive liar

- An average Joe or Jane

54

Get to know one of these characters by imagining him or her in different situations. Choose one situation and start your song with it.

- Someone who is trusting and childlike

- Someone who never gives up

- A cheat

- A hero

55

Choose one of these characters and describe their appearance using details that express who they are. Does she wear a revealing dress because she's trying to be sexy? Does he swagger when he walks because he's an alpha male, the leader of the pack?

- The new girl in school

- Someone who will do anything to win

- A party animal

- The big man on campus

56

What object does this character remind you of? What color, season of the year, type of car? What kind of food, game, type of clothing? Use these in your song lyric.

- A dreamer

- A survivor

- A bully

- A risk taker

58

Choose a character and write a few lyric lines about them. Put that aside and write a short biography. Who are they? What made them the way they are? What hidden conflicts and needs do they have? Now, go back to your lyric and rewrite it. Did you feel you had more to say? Did you understand the character better?

- An optimist

- A pushy salesman

- A straight-A student

- Someone who enjoys making others unhappy

- A joker

58

What happens to other people when this character is around? Make a list of examples. Start a verse lyric with your favorite example. Try to sum up the character's effect with a few choice words at the beginning of the chorus. Go on. You know you want to say it.

- A loser who keeps making bad choices

- A heartbreaker

- A manipulator

- Someone who doesn't notice the harm they cause to others

59

Choose one of these songs and write down the lines you think express the character best. This may be the character of the singer or the person they're singing about. Write a few lines of your own that could replace those. Use them to start a song of your own about a character.

- "Material Girl" – Madonna

- "Mama Tried" – The Everly Brothers

- "Wind Beneath My Wings" – Bette Midler

- "Every Breath You Take" – The Police

- "All About That Bass" – Meghan Trainor

60

What happens when a character falls in love? Telling your audience how this character handles an emotion like love gives listeners a good idea of who they really are. Listen to these two songs to hear examples, and then try it yourself.

- "Better As A Memory" – Kenny Chesney

- "The Man Who Can't Be Moved" – The Script

61

If the singer is the character (as opposed to singing about someone else), would he or she be totally honest? Maybe they would exaggerate their good qualities. Think about how people describe themselves. Choose a character and write what they would say about themselves.

- "We Are The Champions" – Queen

- "Born To Be Wild" – Steppenwolf

- "I'm Too Sexy" – Right Said Fred

- "Life's Been Good" – Joe Walsh

- "Here Comes The Hotstepper" – Ini Kamoze

- "The World's Greatest" – R. Kelly

62

If the singer is the character, be sure the lyric uses the type of language the character would use when speaking. Keep it consistent throughout the song to add credibility. Listen to these two songs, then try a strong, character-driven lyric in a song of your own.

- "Born In The U.S.A." – Bruce Springsteen

- "Suds In The Bucket" – Sara Evans

63

If the singer is describing someone else, what is the singer's relationship to the character? Is this someone they just heard about or someone they know? If it's someone they know, the singer will have more credibility, but both approaches will work.

- "You're So Vain" – Carly Simon

- "Irreplaceable" – Beyoncé

- "Bad, Bad Leroy Brown" – Jim Croce

- "Trouble Child" – Joni Mitchell

- "Englishman In New York" – Sting

64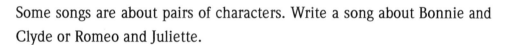

Some songs are about pairs of characters. Write a song about Bonnie and Clyde or Romeo and Juliette.

- "Style" – Taylor Swift

- "Cowboys And Angels" – Dustin Lynch

- "Gasoline And Matches" – Meghan Linsey

65

Listen to these songs and look for the ways they use examples, actions, and situations to express character. Try some of these techniques in a song of your own.

- "One In Every Crowd" – Montgomery Gentry

- "Rhiannon" – Fleetwood Mac

- "She's Leaving Home" – The Beatles

66

Here's an interesting approach to character writing: The singer takes on the character's point of view, even though listeners know the singer is not the character. A good example is "Luka" by Suzanna Vega.

» START WITH AN EMOTION

Most songs are about feelings. It's what songs are really good at — describing, communicating, and making us feel emotions. But how do you write about an emotion? Simply saying "I love you" over and over seldom has much impact. It *tells* listeners what you feel, but it doesn't make them feel it, which is what you want your song to do.

Your aim as a songwriter is to make listeners feel what you feel. The fact that you felt an emotion while writing your song doesn't mean it's automatically communicated to the listener. For that, we use lyric craft — images, actions, physical sensations, comparisons, and associations to make sure listeners get the emotional message at the heart of a song.

In life, emotions are seldom clear and focused, but in songs they always are. In songs, we can love someone with undiluted devotion even if, in reality, we have a few doubts about them. In the Song Starters that follow, I'll give you tips and suggestions for expressing emotions in ways that listeners can feel and understand.

LOVE: FALLING IN LOVE, BEING IN LOVE, LOYALTY, CARING

Love can be many things. Choose the kind of love you want to write about (relationship, family, friends, etc.) then use these Song Starters to help you create words and phrases that will get your lyric started. You can write about the feeling of love itself, or you can write about falling in love, being in a lasting love relationship, a family bond, or a great friendship.

67

Why is love important to you? Why do you want to write a song about that feeling? Listen to these four songs and notice the way they answer the question of love's importance. Try one of those approaches in a lyric of your own.

- "The Power Of Love" – Huey Lewis & the News
- "The First Time Ever I Saw Your Face" – Roberta Flack
- "I'm Yours" – Jason Mraz
- "Try A Little Tenderness" – Otis Redding

68

List three objects that love makes you think of. Choose one and write about why you associate it with love. If you're not satisfied with your answer, try again or move on to the next object. Write a verse or chorus lyric using one of the objects on your list.

69

List three things you would do for someone you love. Use one of them to start a verse or chorus lyric.

70

If love were a sound, what sound would it be? If caring were a smell or a taste, what would it smell like or taste like? If you could touch it, what would it feel like? Use one of those senses in your lyric about love.

71

If love were a season, a month, or time of day, what season, month or time of day would it be? What does that look and feel like?

72

Compare love to an animal. What animal would it be? How does it behave? Is it tame or wild? What does it look like? How does it move? What does it sound like and feel like? Use some of your answers or in a verse or chorus.

73

What color is love? What objects, images, or physical sensations do you associate with that color? Make a list of them. Then make a list of words that are associated with those, and so on. When you have made a few lists, choose the objects, images or sensations that you feel express the emotion effectively and start your lyric.

74

Finish these sentences:

- Love, I want to tell you _____.
- Love makes me_____.
- I never thought I'd _____ for love.

75

What qualities make love last a long time? How does a lasting love feel different from a new love? Write a song about a long-lasting love.

76

What are some of the physical effects of falling in love? How does it make your body feel? Make a list. Use something on your list to start a lyric.

77

These three songs describe the physical effects of falling in love. Listen to the songs, and then write an original verse or chorus lyric that does something similar.

- "Bubbly" – Colbie Caillat

- "Walking On Sunshine" – Katrina and the Waves

- "Smile" – Uncle Kracker

78

Look for more songs that focus on the emotion you want to write about. Read the lyrics. What images, actions, objects, or dialogue lines are used to convey the emotion to you as a listener? Try using something similar to start a song of your own.

SADNESS: HEARTBREAK, LONELINESS, DEPRESSION, GRIEF, YEARNING, REGRET

There's a whole range of dark, sorrowful emotions. Songs based on these feelings can be very expressive and connect strongly with listeners. Keep in mind that these songs don't necessarily cause the listener to feel sad. They might be comforting, helping listeners feel that they're not alone.

79

The following songs express lost love and heartbreak through images and actions. Write a few original lines that you could substitute for some of the lyrics in the song. Use your lines to start a song of your own.

- "You've Lost That Lovin' Feelin'" – The Righteous Brothers

- "Barely Breathing" – Duncan Sheik

- "Ain't No Sunshine" – Bill Withers

- "The Dance" – Garth Brooks

- "I Can't Make You Love Me" – Bonnie Raitt

80

If sorrow were a season or time of day, which season or time of day would it be? What does that look and feel like? Write a lyric about that.

81

What does sadness sound like? The sound of a tear falling on a pillow? Describe the sound of sadness and use it in a chorus lyric.

82

If heartbreak were a food, a kind of music, or an article of clothing, what kind of food, music, or clothing would it be? Describe it. Use some of these words in a verse or chorus.

83

If disappointment were a place, what would it look like? Who would be there? How would you get there or leave? Describe the place in a verse lyric and your feelings about it in a chorus. *(Example: "Heartbreak Hotel" – Elvis Presley)*

84

What color is sadness? What objects, images, or physical sensations do you associate with that color? Make a list. Then make a list of images and words that are associated with those. When you've made your lists, choose the objects, images, or sensations that are most expressive for you and start your lyric.

85

Finish these sentences and let them inspire some lyric ideas:

- Late at night when _____.

- I feel so _____ and it makes me want to _____.

- If I could only_____.

86

List three things that sadness makes you want to do. Use one of them to start a verse or chorus lyric.

87

Here are two songs that deal with grief and loneliness. "I Drive Your Truck" describes real actions the singer takes to deal with grief, while "Hold Back the River" uses a metaphorical action to try to deal with loss. Imagine a real or metaphorical action you could take to deal with one of these emotions and build a song around it.

- "I Drive Your Truck" – Lee Brice

- "Hold Back The River" – James Bay

88

Look for more songs with sorrowful emotions at their core and read the lyrics. What images, actions, objects, or dialogue lines are used to convey the emotion to you as a listener? Try doing something similar to start a song of your own.

HAPPINESS: JOY, WELL-BEING, ELATION, CONTENTMENT, RELIEF

You can write songs about the sheer joy of feeling alive or about anything that makes you happy — family, vacation, partying, a good day on the job, or dreams coming true. So, let's take a look at how images, actions, comparisons, and examples express upbeat feelings to an audience.

89

Listen to the following songs. How do they express happiness or contentment in a way that makes you feel what the singer is feeling? Write a few lyric lines that could replace some of their lines and still express the feeling. Use some of your lines to start a song of your own.

- "Happy" – Pharrell Williams

- "Do You Believe In Magic" – The Lovin' Spoonful

- "What A Wonderful World" – Louis Armstrong

- "Best Day Of Your Life" – Katie Herzig

- "Beautiful Day" – Joshua Radin

- "Enjoy Yourself" – Billy Currington

90

We express our emotions in the way we walk, talk, and move. Describe the way you walk when you feel elated. Describe your "happy dance." Write a verse or chorus lyric and include some of those words.

91

What does laughter look like? What does a smile sound like?

92

What does happiness taste like? Describe the taste. Fill a verse lyric with the taste of happiness.

93

If happiness were a season, which one would it be? What does that season look and feel like?

94

What color is happiness? What objects, images, or physical sensations do you associate with that color? Make a list. Then make a list of images and words that are associated with those. When you've made a few lists, choose the objects, images, or sensations that are most expressive for you and start your lyric.

95

Make a list of events, objects, and people that make you happy. Use some of these in a verse or chorus lyric.

96

If happiness were an animal, what animal would it be? How does it move when it's happy? Does it make a sound? Use some of the words in your answers to describe how you feel when you're happy.

97

Finish these sentences and let them inspire a lyric idea:

- I'm so happy I could _____.
- Every time _____ I just have to smile.
- The most fun I've ever had was _____.

98

Look for more songs with this emotion at their core and read the lyrics. What images, actions, objects, or dialogue lines are used to convey the emotion to you as a listener? Try doing something similar to start a song of your own.

ANGER: FRUSTRATION, REVENGE, CONTEMPT, DISLIKE, HATE

While there are some very successful songs written about anger, this is an emotion that can easily put listeners off if you're not careful. Anger can sound like whining or bullying if the audience doesn't feel the singer's resentment is justified. You don't need to include specific details, just give enough information to let listeners in on the situation.

99

Listen to the following songs. How do they express anger, dislike, or revenge? How do you know what the singer is feeling? Is that feeling justified in the song's lyric? Write a few original lyric lines that could replace some of these lines and still express the feeling. Use your lines to start new songs of your own.

- "Stronger (What Doesn't Kill You)" – Kelly Clarkson
- "King Of Anything" – Sara Bareilles
- "Take A Bow" – Rihanna
- "Before He Cheats" – Carrie Underwood
- "Bully" – Shinedown
- "Pumped Up Kicks" – Foster The People
- "Gangsta's Paradise" – Coolio

100

Make a list of phrases that describe the way you walk and talk when you're angry. Use some of these words in your lyric.

101

What kind of behavior or type of person makes you angry? Is that anger justified? How do you show your anger?

102

If anger were a sound, what sound would it be? Use that sound. Describe it in a verse or chorus lyric.

103

If anger were a smell or a taste, what would it be? Describe the smell or the taste. Use words from your description in a song about feeling angry.

104

If anger were a storm, what kind of storm would it be? What does the storm look like? When you are caught in it, how does it feel?

105

List at least three physical responses you have when you're angry. Start a verse or chorus with one of them.

106

Imagine anger as an animal. What animal is it? What sound does it make? What does it look like? How does it move? What does it feel like? Use some of your answers in a verse or chorus.

107

List three objects that anger makes you think of. Use one of them in a lyric.

108

What color is anger? What objects, images, or physical sensations do you associate with that color? Make a list. Then make a list of images and words that are associated with those. When you have a couple lists, choose the objects, images, or sensations that are most expressive for you and start your lyric.

109 🍃

Finish these sentences:

- I'm so mad I could _____.

- I won't be your victim anymore. I'll _____.

- You shouldn't have _____. Now I'm going to _____.

110 🍃

Look for more songs with this emotion at the core and read the lyrics. What images, actions, objects, or dialogue lines are used to convey the emotion to you as a listener? Try using something similar to start a song of your own.

MORE EMOTIONS TO WRITE ABOUT...

There are many more emotions you can write about in addition to the Big Four we've looked at here. Listen to some of the song examples below, and then adapt the questions in the previous Song Starters on Love, Sadness, Happiness, and Anger to the feeling you want to write about.

JEALOUSY: ENVY, GREED, DESIRE FOR CONTROL

- "Every Breath You Take" – The Police

- "Jessie's Girl" – Rick Springfield

- "The Boy Is Mine" – Brandy & Monica
- "Run For Your Life" – The Beatles

FEAR: WORRY, ANXIETY, PANIC

- "Afraid" – Nelly Furtado
- "How Far We've Come" – Matchbox Twenty
- "Eve Of Destruction" – Barry McGuire

EXCITEMENT: ANTICIPATION, EAGERNESS, SURPRISE

- "I Gotta Feeling" – The Black Eyed Peas
- "Anticipation" – Carly Simon
- "After Hours" – We Are Scientists
- "Good Time" – Owl City

COURAGE: CONFIDENCE, PRIDE, OPTIMISM, HOPE

- "Fight Song" – Rachel Platten
- "Roar" – Katy Perry
- "Standing Outside The Fire" – Garth Brooks
- "Beautiful" – Christina Aguilera
- "Eye Of The Tiger" – Survivor
- "Brave" – Sara Bareilles

» START WITH A TITLE

A good song title can kickstart your creative ideas and keep your theme on track as you write. It can provide raw material and inspiration as you work your way through each song section, and it can stay in the listener's head long after the song is over. These are just a few of the reasons many pro songwriters start with a song title first. While there are plenty of other ways to start a song — you're holding a book full of them — working from a title is a proven winner and well worth a try.

If you aren't already keeping a list of potential song titles, now is a good time to start. As you go through the Song Starters in this section, you'll be writing *a lot* of titles. Be sure to keep a list of the titles you create. Put your list someplace where you can easily get to it when you want to add to it or use it. When you're ready to write a song and need a little inspiration, your title list will be waiting.

<u>NOTE:</u> In this section, I'll be giving you examples of hit song titles. While a title cannot be copyrighted, it's a good idea to avoid using highly recognizable hit song titles for your own songs. If you happen to come up with a title that's the same as a well-known hit song, try changing a few words to give it your own original stamp.

KEEP IT SHORT

Listeners recall short phrases more easily than long ones. From one word to five or six words is a good length. When your title is used in your song, you can always make it part of a longer phrase.

111

Take a look at the current radio airplay charts at Billboard.com or BDSradio.com. What length are most of the titles? For practice, write a few titles similar to some that you find on the charts. If you come up with a title you like, start a song with it.

112

Write a sentence of eight to twelve words (or more). In the phrase, describe something you feel like doing or saying when you're happy. When you're done, shorten it to six words or less. Preserve the meaning of your phrase while subtracting anything you don't absolutely need.

113

Write a sentence of eight or more words describing something you do or say when you feel sad or angry. Then shorten it to five words or less, preserving the essential meaning of the phrase.

114

Write a short phrase of one to six words, or use one of these: "Got To Let It Go," "Hanging On To You," "Been There." Write a few lines describing what a song with that title might be about. What kind of situation would the singer be in? Is there someone else involved? Is there something the singer wants to do or to avoid? If you come up with an idea that interests you, start a song lyric.

USE IMAGES IN YOUR TITLE

When you use an image in your title, you evoke a mental picture for the listener. Images are often easier to recall and have a bigger impact than abstract ideas. Here are some examples of hit song titles that use images. Notice how each one evokes a mental picture.

- "Halo" – Beyoncé
- "Chandelier" – Sia
- "Pocketful Of Sunshine" – Natasha Bedingfield
- "Candle In The Wind" – Elton John
- "The Long And Winding Road" – The Beatles
- "Mud On The Tires" – Brad Paisley

115

Write a title using one or more of these images: star, sky, rain, hands, smile, home, tears, angel, truck. Write your title on a piece of paper and make a list of other images and ideas it suggests. Use these as raw material to start your lyric.

116

Write a title using one or more of these pictures: money, bank, heart, boy, girl, dance, sunshine, clouds. Write your title down followed by a few phrases that describe the image. Add more images and ideas of your own. Don't worry about rhyme — just write.

117

Write a title using any image you like. Make a list of questions listeners might have about your title. For example: What does the title mean? Why is this important to the singer? What's happening? How does the singer feel about it? Write a chorus that includes your title and answers one of the questions.

118

Write a title using one or more of these images: beach, summer night, fast car, road, T-shirt, dress, fire, sand, eyes, arms. Write a one-sentence description of what a song with that title might be about. Answer any questions you think listeners might have, like: Why did the singer do that? How does the singer feel about what's happening? Write a chorus that expresses the heart of your idea. Use the title at least once.

119

Make a list of images you might like to use in a title. Choose images you feel drawn to, ones that suggest something you'd like to write about. Select one of the images on your list and use it in a title. Create a one-sentence description of what a song with that title might be about. Write a chorus lyric using your title at least once.

USE ACTION WORDS IN YOUR TITLE

Get your listeners involved in the energy and action of your song right from the start. These hit song titles use motion and momentum words:

- "Collide" – Howie Day

- "Crash My Party" – Luke Bryan

- "Chasing Cars" – Snow Patrol

- "Dancing In The Street" – Martha and the Vandellas

In other hit song titles, you'll find actions that involve speaking ("apologize," "say"), physical interaction ("hold," "kiss," "hit"), stopping ("stay," "stand"), and more. Here are a few examples:

- "Apologize" – OneRepublic

- "Say You Do" – Dierks Bentley

- "Hold Me" – Fleetwood Mac

- "Hit Me With Your Best Shot" — Pat Benatar

- "Stay With Me" – Sam Smith

- "Stand By Me" – Ben E. King

120

Write as many titles as you can using these action words: spin, slide, fall, fly, slip, drop, climb, rise. Adapt as needed, for example "spin," "spinning," "spins." When you have a few titles, choose one and write a one-sentence song idea. Expand your title into a chorus using your title at least once.

121

Create a short list of titles using these action words: shout, cry, call, say, laugh, talk, scream, roar, whisper, sigh. You can adapt a word if needed, for example "cry," "crying," "cries." When you have a few titles, choose the one you like best and write a one-sentence summary of your song idea. Imagine yourself involved in that action. What does it feel like? What kind of situation does it suggest to you? Expand those ideas into a verse and chorus using your title at least once in the chorus.

122

Work up a few titles using these actions: let go, leave, move on, look back, disappear, hold, push, pull, touch, drive, break, shatter. Change any words as needed, such as "leave," "leaving," "leaves." When you have a short list of titles, choose one and write a one-sentence song description for that title. Expand it into a chorus using your title at least once. In your chorus, answer the question: Why am I doing this?

123

Make a list of action words you might like to use in a title. Think of words that involve physical momentum (run, walk, jump), speaking (whisper, yell), stopping (stay, hang on), or any action you like. Choose one and use it in a title. Imagine the questions listeners might ask about that title and answer them in your lyric.

MAKE A BOLD OR INTRIGUING STATEMENT

Tabloid headlines are brilliant at grabbing attention. And a good song title should do the same. For example, imagine this spread across the front page of The National Enquirer: "OOPS! I DID IT AGAIN!" SQUEALS BRITNEY. Song titles often imply a juicy situation, one with plenty of drama and emotion. You can try writing "title headlines" yourself. Here are a few more examples to give you some ideas.

- BEATLES TROUBLED, NEED "HELP!"

- "GIRLS JUST WANT TO HAVE FUN!" WHINES CYNDI LAUPER.

- ROBERTA FLACK CRIES "WHERE IS THE LOVE?!!"

- TIM MCGRAW HURTING. SAYS "HIGHWAY DON'T CARE."

Now it's your turn to write a tabloid headline and create a title.

124 ✎

Finish this sentence: JUSTIN BIEBER SWEARS "I NEVER _____!"
Use the quote as your song title and start your chorus lyric with it.

125 ✎

Finish this headline: KATY PERRY ADMITS, "I COULD _____."
Make the quote your song title and use it in a chorus lyric.

126

KANYE WEST WORRIED. "I NEED _____!"
Turn the quote into a song title. Answer the questions listeners might have.

127

BLAKE SHELTON LAMENTS: "I'VE GOT _____!"
Use the quote as your song title and write a chorus featuring the title.

128

TAYLOR SWIFT GOES BALLISTIC. "IT'S NOT _____!!!"
Turn the quote into a song title and answer the questions inquiring minds
are sure to have.

129

Choose any famous recording artist you like and write the artist's name
in headline capital letters. Follow that with the word "says" or "cries" or
"shouts." Then write a statement, question, or comment. Use what you
wrote as a title. If you like it, add it to your title list and use it in a chorus.

130

Check out an online tabloid website, or pick up a copy of any tabloid or
celebrity news magazine. Look through the headlines for title ideas.

131 🖉

Imagine a paparazzi photo of a celeb in a candid moment. Write the headline and turn it into a song title.

QUESTIONS MAKE GOOD TITLES, TOO

A title with a question mark demands an answer and listeners will stick around to find out what it is. In some titles, these are real, heartfelt questions; in others they're rhetorical questions, meaning the singer already knows the answer. Here are a few examples of each:

- "How Deep Is Your Love?" – Bee Gees
- "What Do You Mean?" – Justin Bieber
- "Do You Really Want To Hurt Me?" – Culture Club
- "What Was I Thinkin'" – Dierks Bentley
- "What's Love Got To Do With It?" – Tina Turner

132 🖉

Write three or four titles in the form of a question. Imagine an emotionally charged situation in which one person is trying to understand what's going on. What questions would he or she ask? Work those questions into a lyric.

133 ✦

Try writing a couple of titles that are rhetorical questions. They either have an obvious answer or don't require an answer at all. A good way to come up with these questions is to imagine yourself in an angry or emotional confrontation with someone else. Rhetorical questions like "What do I have to do to get some respect?!!" or "What's your problem?!!" are sure to pop up.

134 ✦

Ask a question in eight words or less. Write it down and use it as the first line of a chorus lyric. In the rest of the chorus either answer the question or make it clear that the singer already knows the answer.

135 ✦

Ask the question, "What happened to us?" Imagine an emotional situation in which one person asks another person that question. Work up a verse lyric that describes what led up to the question ("We used to…" "You used to…"). Start or end your chorus with the question and, in between, describe the singer's feelings about it.

USE WORDS WITH EMOTIONAL ASSOCIATIONS

Some words have extra layers of feelings associated with them. They're easily recognized as happy (sunny, warm, smile), sad (cold, lost, cry), or angry (storm, fist, shout). Of course, the context in which the word is used makes a big difference, but you can count on these words to evoke some kind of emotion in your listener depending on how you use them.

Here are a few examples of hit song titles that use words with strong emotional associations. These words telegraph the central feeling of the song.

- "Walking On Sunshine" – Katrina and the Waves
- "Daydream" – The Lovin' Spoonful
- "Fight Song" – Rachel Platten
- "The Tracks Of My Tears" – Smokey Robinson & the Miracles
- "Winter" – Joshua Radin

136

Here are a few words with strong emotional associations. Write a title using one or more of these words to increase its emotional impact. If you like your title, use it as the first or last line of a chorus lyric.

- river, rain, drown, flood, swept away, lost, alone

137

Write a title using one or more of these words to increase the emotional impact. If you like your title, rough out a verse or chorus lyric using more of the words in this list and other words they suggest to you.

- heat, dry, dust, empty, thirsty, hungry, need, want, desire

138

Work up a strong, emotional title using one or more of these words. If you like your title, rough out a verse or chorus lyric using more of the words in this list and other words they suggest to you.

- winter, cold, moon, dark, storm, tears, lose, fall, stumble

139

These words have uplifting emotional associations. Write a title with one or more of them and use it as the first or last line of a chorus. Fill in the rest of the chorus with lines that describe what the singer is feeling.

- angel, heart, hope, halo, dream, lift, reach, hold on, fly, rise

140

Look through lists of hit song titles for words that are frequently featured. These are the ones that tend to have that extra layer of emotion. You can find lists of song titles online by searching the internet for "top 100 songs" or "best songs." Make a list of words that you find appealing, words you'd like to use in a title. Try out a few of those in short phrases. Choose one and feature it in a chorus lyric.

USE A CONVERSATIONAL TITLE

Sometimes a title is simply an honest statement, direct and uncompli-cated. The very simplicity of these titles makes them seem believable and authentic, as if the singer just thought of the words.

- "I Will Always Love You" – Whitney Houston

- "Let Her Go" – Passenger

- "We Are Never Ever Getting Back Together" – Taylor Swift

- "Need You Now" – Lady Antebellum

- "You're Beautiful" – James Blunt

141

Write three short phrases (six words or less) that you might say to someone you've just fallen in love with. Use one to start your chorus lyric.

142

You feel betrayed. Write three short phrases (six words or less) you might say to someone who has done you wrong. Use one to end a chorus lyric.

143

You want to end a relationship. Write three short phrases (six words or less) you might say to someone you've decided to break up with. Use one or more in a chorus lyric.

144

You're faced with a life-changing challenge. Write three short phrases (six words or less) you might say to give yourself strength and reassurance. Use one or more in a chorus lyric.

145

You have a friend or loved one who's in trouble. Write three short phrases (six words or less) to let that person know you'll be there for them no matter what. Write a chorus lyric based on these lines.

FOUND TITLES

Sometimes you don't have to look for a title — a title finds you. All you need to do is recognize it. While reading, watching TV, or cruising the internet, keep your eyes and ears open. Look for stories and scenes about relationships, break ups, getting back together, and overcoming challenges. Listen for short phrases and write them down using title capitalization. On a recent expedition, I found: "White-Hot Love," "I'm Recovering," "It's Only a Game," and "I Feel Blessed." If you find something that isn't exactly right but suggests an idea, go ahead and rewrite it until you like it. Now, try your luck.

146

Skim through celebrity news magazines like *People* and *Us.* (They have websites as well as print editions.) Find three words or phrases that could work as song titles. Choose one and work it into a chorus lyric.

147

Watch an episode of a TV drama. Shows with emotional interaction between characters will work better than action shows. Listen for words and phrases that could work as titles and write them down. See how many you can find. Use one to start a chorus lyric.

148

Check out TV talk shows (afternoon or late night). Listen for quotes and quips you can turn into song titles and use one in a lyric.

149

Eavesdrop on conversations. Listen to yourself when you're talking to someone. Look for words and phrases you can turn into titles. Even Bob Dylan admits he does this.

WRITE A TITLE FOR A TV COMMERCIAL SONG

Songs for TV commercials have a special job to do. They reach out to the viewer and deliver an emotional message in conjunction with a product or brand. Gone are the days of hard-sell jingles. Today's TV commercials feature songs with an authentic emotional core centered on feelings of happiness, togetherness, optimism, positive change, and new beginnings.

150

Picture this common commercial: a reunion with plenty of hugs, lots of good food, laughter, and old friends. Write a phrase that sums up the feeling. Use it as a song title. Add a few more lines that describe the emotions that bring people together and start a lyric.

151

Picture this typical ad: a mom or dad driving home in a new car, being greeted with shouts of excitement by children and neighbors. Write a title that sums up the feeling you get when you buy something new, something you really want. Feature your title in a short refrain-style chorus, just a couple of repeated lines.

152

Here's an ad you see a lot: Imagine a celebration, a birthday or anniversary with friends and family sharing in the happiness and fun. Write a phrase that expresses the emotions in that moment. Make a list of images and action words you could use to fill out your lyric. Feature your phrase in a short chorus and write a brief verse with your images and action words.

BUILD A SONG ON YOUR TITLE

Now that you have a long list of great titles, how do you turn them into songs? I've been giving hints throughout this section, but here are a few exercises that will show you how to do it.

NOTE: Where there is no artist name following a title, you can go ahead and use it. I created these titles for you. A few of them have appeared in songs, but none in well-known hits, at least none so far. So, go ahead and write one.

153

Look through the following titles. Pick one and describe in one sentence what the song might be about. Write down the emotion you want to express in the song. Make a list of images, action words, ideas, and phrases the title and emotion suggest to you. List some examples of what the singer does to express his or her feelings. When you have enough raw material, start putting a lyric together that features the title in a prominent spot, like the beginning or end of the chorus. As you work, keep adding to your lists of images and action words.

- "Walking Home Without You"

- "What's Stopping Us?"

- "If I Say It"

- "I'll Be Standing Here"

- "Maybe It Will Rain"

154

Write a title of your own and describe what your song will be about in one sentence. Decide what emotion you want to express in the song. Make a list of images, action words, ideas, and phrases the title and emotion suggest. Think about what the singer would say or do to express those feelings. Work up a lyric that features your title in a prominent place. Consider using examples in the verses and the most emotional lines in your chorus. Keep adding images, action words, and examples as you think of them.

155

Choose one of these titles and make a list of questions you'd like to answer in your song along with any questions you think listeners might have. Try answering questions like: How does the singer feel about this? What has happened to make the singer feel this way? What does the title mean or why is it important? What do you think will happen next? Answer one of these questions in your chorus and others in your verses and bridge section.

- "What I Want to Say"

- "It's Closer Than You Think"

- "I Can't Be the One"

- "Save a Place for You"

156

Write a title of your own and make a list of questions you'd like to answer in your song. Include a few questions you think listeners will have. Answer at least one question in each section of your song lyric.

157

Changing one word in your title can suggest a whole new song. Pick one or more of these titles and write down what you think the song will be about. Then change a word or add or subtract a word. Write down what you think the song might be about after you make the changes.

- "A Steady Heart"
- "Change (Can Be A Good Thing)"
- "Chasing Dreams"
- "Not The Next Time"
- "There's Never A Good Time"

158

Go through your list of titles, or use the titles in this section, and change, add, or subtract any word. Notice how the new title changes the core idea of the song. Keep any title that sounds like it has potential. Choose any of your changed titles and write a lyric.

» START WITH A CLICHÉ

Clichés are everywhere. These banal, overly-familiar lines even creep into our song lyrics. But that's not necessarily a bad thing. You can use a cliché to your advantage if you twist it, change the meaning, or make it mean something more. Here are a few examples of songs that use clichés successfully. Look up the lyrics to see how the cliché was handled.

- "Nick Of Time" – Bonnie Raitt

- "On The Other Hand" – Randy Travis

- "Cry Me A River" – Julie London

- "Dirty Laundry" – Don Henley

- "I'd Do Anything For Love (But I Won't Do That)" – Meat Loaf

- "Anything Goes" – Frank Sinatra

- "Heart Of Gold" – Neil Young

- "Hit The Road, Jack" – Ray Charles

- "I Heard It Through The Grapevine" – Marvin Gaye

- "You're Gonna Miss This" – Trace Adkins

159

Write a song about two people who are "as different as night and day." Think about this cliché phrase and write down your own interpretation of it. What does it really mean? What's different about night and day? Aren't night and day also connected in important ways?

160

What does "No pain, no gain" really mean? How could you apply it to a relationship? Think of other ways to express this idea. Start a verse with one of those.

161

What does "Stop and smell the roses" mean? When and why should people do that? Have you ever felt stressed out and then taken a break? How did it feel to relax and enjoy life again? Write a song about that. Find different ways to tell people to "stop and smell the roses."

162

What do we mean when we say "He who hesitates is lost"? Apply that to something that happened in your life and write about it.

163

Tell someone why you don't want to be "out of sight, out of mind." What will you do, and how far will you go to make sure that doesn't happen?

164

Are the best things in life really free? Try approaching that idea from an unexpected angle.

165

Is it true that "The more you get, the more you want"? What kinds of things make you feel that way? You could write a song about greed that's good (wanting more good lovin'), or greed that's bad (a person who is never satisfied with anything). Or something completely different. Come up with a fresh angle and go for it.

166

"Time heals all wounds," even wounds of the heart, but it doesn't always feel that way. What are your feelings about this phrase? Have you found it to be true? What would you say to yourself or someone who is hurting?

167

"What you don't know can't hurt you." Or so they say. Think of situations in which what you don't know can hurt you and write a song about it.

168

Think of a reason why someone might say: "You've been talking behind my back." Imagine the situation. Put yourself in it and feel the emotion. Maybe you're the one who's been doing the talking. How does *that* feel? Write a song about the situation and emotions and use the cliché "You've been talking behind my back" in the lyric.

169 ✍

Choose one of the clichés from the following list and write a song that uses it in a way listeners won't expect.

- Better late than never.

- Love is blind.

- Just a bump in the road.

- Home is where the heart is.

170 ✍

Choose a cliché from the following list and extend it with an additional phrase. (Example: "I'd do anything for love… but I won't do that.") Write a song using your new, longer phrase as the first or last line of the chorus.

- Take the easy way out.

- Time slips away.

- Save your breath.

- A heart as cold as ice.

171 ✍

Choose a cliché from this list and change one word to make it mean something new. Write a song about that.

- I'm not buying it.

- You can't teach an old dog new tricks.

- Live like there's no tomorrow.

- I'm wearing my heart on my sleeve.

172

Add a line that turns one of these clichés into an emotional situation you want to write about.

- Kiss and tell.

- It's make or break time.

- A ghost of a chance.

- So close I can taste it.

» START WITH A RHYME

Today's lyrics use a range of rhyming styles. You might hear a "perfect rhyme" like *will/still* right next to a "near rhyme" like *same/train* or *staying/complaining.* Using near rhymes — words that share similar vowel sounds but not the same consonant — can give you more choices when writing and can add interest to your lyrics.

A pair of rhyming lines can suggest a theme or overall idea for your song. Try using some of these rhymes to suggest the direction your entire song might go.

173 🍃

Use *sign/eyes* as a rhyming pair. Let the lines suggest a lyric idea for the rest of your song.

174 🍃

Use *get/step* or *help/else* or both as rhyming pairs. Base your song on a theme suggested by those lines.

175 🍃

Use *room/soon* or *touch/enough* or both as rhyming pairs. What lyric theme do these lines suggest?

176

Use some of these near rhymes — *same/save/afraid/face/late* — in a verse or chorus and follow up on the situation your lines suggest.

177

Rhyme *love* with *blood, drug, enough, up,* or *hug.* Work up a lyric based on the idea in those lines.

178

Rhyme *illusion* with any of these: *choosin', foolin', doin',* or *tune in.* What lyric idea does that suggest?

179

Rhyme *freedom* with *be one,* or add an extra syllable by using *need someone.* Build your lyric on that idea.

180

Write a verse lyric using the rhyming pair *staying/complaining.*

181

Write a chorus lyric using the rhyming pair *breathing/believing.*

182

Write a verse lyric using the rhyming pair *saying it/faking it.*

183

Start a lyric using some of these rhymes *reason/uneven/sweeten/deceivin'.*

PART TWO

SONG STARTERS: CHORDS

Many of today's biggest hits rely on basic three- and four-chord progressions. These kinds of generic progressions are not copyrighted; they've been used in dozens of hit songs. That means you can use them, too. On the following pages, you'll find many of these familiar chord progressions. You can use them "as is" or change them any way you like. Repeat them as many times as you need to. Substitute a different chord. Transpose them up or down. Add an intro or an ending or a transition chord.

I've included hit song examples for the most common progressions so you can hear how they're used. When you write a song using one of these progressions, be sure you *only* use the chords. The hit song melody, lyrics, and instrumental arrangement are copyrighted.

If you don't play an instrument, look for a karaoke version of the example song on iTunes or a website like Karaoke-version.com.

SONG STARTERS

» START WITH A THREE-CHORD PROGRESSION

184

Choose one of the three-chord progressions in this section and play it at any speed or with any rhythm you like. As you play, let the progression suggest a melody or lyric idea. You can sing whatever occurs to you, or use a lyric you created in the Lyric Starters section. Try this with a few of the progressions. When you find something you like, record it.

185

Listen to a three-chord hit song like "The Tide Is High" by Blondie or "All About That Bass" by Meghan Trainor. Play along with the recording. (The chords are included in the list of three-chord progressions that follows.) Write an original melody and lyric to the same chords. If your first try is too close to the hit song, change the rhythm and pitch of the melody notes until you have something more unique.

186

Choose one of the three-chord progressions included in this section and double the length of one of the chords. Or double the length of *all* of the chords. Write a melody to your new progression.

187

Use one of three-chord progressions in this section, but change the order of the chords. Start with the last chord in the progression or start with the middle chord.

188

Select one of these three-chord progressions and replace one of the chords with a chord of your choosing. Write a melody and lyric to your new progression. Consider using the hit song progression in some song sections. You could write a verse with one progression, a chorus with the other.

THREE-CHORD PROGRESSION 1

| A | D E | – Repeat.

Four beats on A, then two beats each on D and E.

Example: "The Tide Is High" – Blondie

To play along, capo on the 2nd fret or transpose your keyboard +2.

THREE-CHORD PROGRESSION 2

| D G | A | – Repeat.

Two beats each on D and G, then four beats on A.

Example: "What Makes You Beautiful" – One Direction

To play along, capo on the 2nd fret or transpose your keyboard +2.

THREE-CHORD PROGRESSION 3

| G | G | Amin | Amin | D | D | G | G | – Repeat.

Example: "All About That Bass" – Meghan Trainor

To play along, capo on the 2nd fret or transpose your keyboard +2.

THREE-CHORD PROGRESSION 4

| D | E A | – Repeat.
Four beats on D. Two beats each on E and A.

Example: "Live to Be Free" – Griffin House

To play along, capo on the 1st fret or transpose your keyboard +1.

THREE-CHORD PROGRESSION 5

| Emin C | D | – Repeat.
Two beats each on Emin and C. Four beats on D.

Example: "Bottoms Up" – Brantley Gilbert

THREE-CHORD PROGRESSION 6

| C | G | F | G | – Repeat.

Example: "Truly, Madly, Deeply" – Savage Garden

THREE-CHORD PROGRESSION 7

| G | G | C | C | Emin | Emin | C | C | – Repeat.

Example: "I Gotta Feeling" – The Black Eyed Peas

THREE-CHORD PROGRESSION 8

| Amin F | C | – Repeat.

Two beats each on Amin and F. Four beats on C.

Example: "Stay With Me" – Sam Smith

THREE-CHORD PROGRESSION 9

| G | C | – Repeat.

| Amin | C | – Use as a turnaround as needed.

Example: "Technicolor" – Tim Myers

THREE-CHORD PROGRESSION 10

| G | G | Amin | Amin | C | C | G | G | – Repeat.

Example: "Don't Worry, Be Happy" – Bobby McFerrin

To play along, capo on the 4th fret or transpose your keyboard +4.

THREE-CHORD PROGRESSION 11

| D | Amin | Amin | Emin | – Repeat.

Example: "Clocks" – Coldplay (verse & chorus)

To play along, capo on the 1st fret or transpose your keyboard +1.

» START WITH A FOUR-CHORD PROGRESSION

189 ✎

Play one of the four-chord progressions in this section and repeat it several times using any rhythm or tempo you like. As you play, let the progression suggest a melody or lyric idea. Sing it a few times, then add another line. Don't worry about rhyming. Just sing whatever occurs to you. Try adding a couple more lines. Record your idea. Use some of the melody pattern or lyric Song Starters in this book to work on your song.

190 ✎

Play one of the four-chord progressions on the list in this section. Repeat it several times as you record it to a steady beat. Play back the recording and write a melody and lyric to the chords. Writing to a recording can give you more freedom to be inventive with your melody. Consider starting your melody on an unusual beat or at different places in the progression.

Explore what happens when you do that. When you hear something you like, work on it.

191 ✎

Listen to a successful four-chord song like the Country hit "Highway Don't Care" by Tim McGraw or John Legend's "All Of Me." Play along with the recording. (The chords are included in the list that follows.) Write an original melody and lyric to the same chords. If your first try is too close to the hit song, change the rhythm and pitch of the melody notes until you have something more original. Change lyric lines by using different images, action words, or examples.

192

Pick one of the four-chord progressions included in this section and double the length of one of the chords. Cut the length in half on the next two chords. Write a melody to your new progression. You can try this with any four-chord progression. You'll get a new progression that sounds quite different.

193

Use one of the four-chord progressions in the following list as the basis for a song, but change the order of the chords. Start with the last chord in the progression, or start in the middle.

194

Select one of the following four-chord progressions and replace one of the chords with another chord of your choosing. Write a melody and lyric using the hit song progression in the verse and your new progression in the chorus.

FOUR-CHORD PROGRESSION 1

| G | D | Emin | C | – Repeat.

Examples: "I'm Yours" – Jason Mraz,

"Collide" – Howie Day, and many more.

To play along, capo on the 4th fret or transpose your keyboard +4.

FOUR-CHORD PROGRESSION 2

| D | Bmin | G | A | – Repeat.

Example: "Highway Don't Care" – Tim McGraw

FOUR-CHORD PROGRESSION 3

| G | Amin | Emin | C | – Repeat.

Example: "Halo" – Beyoncé

To play along, capo on the 2nd fret or transpose your keyboard +2.

FOUR-CHORD PROGRESSION 4

| Emin | C | G | D | – Repeat.

Examples: "All Of Me" – John Legend

To play along, capo on the 1st fret or transpose your keyboard +1.

FOUR-CHORD PROGRESSION 5

| Amin | C | G | F | – Repeat.

Example: "Counting Stars" – OneRepublic

To play along, capo on the 4th fret or transpose your keyboard +4.

FOUR-CHORD PROGRESSION 6

| C | Emin | Amin | F | – Repeat.

Example: "Like I'm Gonna Lose You" – Meghan Trainor w/John Legend

FOUR-CHORD PROGRESSION 7

| C | G | Dmin | F | – Repeat.

Example: The chorus of "Almost Lover" – A Fine Frenzy

» START WITH A PROGRESSION IN SONG FORM

The progressions in this section are laid out in song form, with a verse and chorus and sometimes a pre-chorus or bridge.

195

Choose one of the song progressions in this section. Play the progression a few times at any tempo or with any rhythm you like. When you're comfortable with it, record it, and then write a melody and lyric using the song layout as a guide.

196

Use one of the song progressions included in the list that follows and double the length of some of the chords. Cut the length in half on other chords. Write a melody and lyric to your new progression.

197

Select a chord progression from the list in this section and switch the verse and chorus progressions. Or change one of the chords in the progression to a chord that isn't used anywhere else. Record your new progression. Try to get a sense of the emotion in the chords, and then work up a rough lyric and melody that complements it.

198

Select one of the song progressions included in this section and play it a few times. In the verse, start singing melody phrases on the second chord in the progression. In the chorus, start the melody phrases on the first chord in the progression.

199

Choose one of the song progressions in this section and repeat it a few times to get familiar with it. Try a few different rhythm grooves: Play it as a slow ballad or in a spinning waltz rhythm (3/4 or 6/8). Try a Latin feel or a Country or Rock style. Add a drum or percussion loop if you want. As you play, let the rhythmic feel suggest a melody or lyric idea. When you find something you like, record it and build on that.

SONG PROGRESSION 1

VERSE: | A | D | – Repeat.

PRE-CHORUS: | E | Bmin | E | Bmin | E | E |

CHORUS: | A | D | A | E | A | D | A | E | E |

Example: "Glory Days" – Bruce Springsteen (similar)

SONG PROGRESSION 2

VERSE: | Amin | G | F | G | – Repeat.

PRE-CHORUS: | F | G | – Repeat.

CHORUS: | Amin | G | F | G | – Repeat.

Example: "Dreams" – Fleetwood Mac (similar)

SONG PROGRESSION 3

VERSE: | Am | F | C | G | – Repeat.

PRE-CHORUS: | Dmin | Dmin | Amin | Amin | F | F | G | G |

CHORUS: | Am | F | C | G | – Repeat.

Example: "Stronger (What Doesn't Kill You)" – Kelly Clarkson (similar)

SONG PROGRESSION 4

VERSE: | C | G | Amin | F | – Repeat.

CHORUS: | F | G | F | G | – Repeat.

Example: "Hey, Soul Sister" – Train (similar)

To play along, capo on the 4th fret or transpose your keyboard +4.

SONG PROGRESSION 5

Stretching out the same chords can create contrast.

VERSE: | E B | A B | – Repeat. (2 beats on each chord)

CHORUS: | E | B | A | E B | – Repeat.

Example: "Chicken Fried" – Zac Brown Band

To play along, capo on the 2nd fret or transpose your keyboard +2.

SONG PROGRESSION 6

VERSE: | Amin | F | G | Emin | – Repeat.

PRE-CHORUS: | F | Amin | G | G | – Repeat.

CHORUS: | F | G | C | F | – Repeat.

Example: "Chandelier" – Sia

To play along, capo on the 1st fret or transpose your keyboard +1.

SONG PROGRESSION 7

A pre-chorus can create contrast between two similar sections.

VERSE: | C | G | Amin | G | – Repeat.

PRE-CHORUS: | Amin | G | – Repeat.

CHORUS: | C | G | Amin | G | – Repeat.

Example: "Fallin' For You" – Colbie Caillat (similar)

To play along, capo on the 4th fret or transpose your keyboard +4.

Once you get the hang of using chord progressions, try some of these. There are no example songs. Just follow the song layout and create your own lyric and melody.

SONG PROGRESSION 8

VERSE: | C | Amin | Emin | G | – Repeat.

CHORUS: | C | G | Amin | F | – Repeat.

BRIDGE: | Dmin | Dmin | G | G | – Repeat if needed.

SONG PROGRESSION 9

VERSE: | G | Emin | – Repeat.

PRE-CHORUS: | C | D | – Repeat.

CHORUS: | G | C | Emin | D | – Repeat.

SONG PROGRESSION 10

VERSE: | Amin | C | G | Dmin | – Repeat.

PRE-CHORUS: | F | Amin | G | G |

CHORUS: | Amin | F | G | F | – Repeat.

SONG PROGRESSION 11

VERSE: | Dmin | Amin | – Repeat.

PRE-CHORUS: | G | Dmin | – Repeat.

CHORUS: | C | Dmin | F | G | – Repeat.

SONG PROGRESSION 12

VERSE: | Cmin | Cmin | Bb | Bb | Fmin | Fmin | Ab | Ab |

PRE-CHORUS: | Ab | Bb | Ab | Bb |

CHORUS: | Cmin | Cmin | Eb | Eb | Bb | Bb | Fmin |

Ab | – Repeat if needed.

BRIDGE: | Bb | Bb | Fmin | Fmin | – Repeat if needed.

200

Listen to one of your favorite songs and play the chord progression. You can learn it by listening to the song or look up the chord progression online. Do an internet search using the song title and the word "chords." Use part or all of the chord progression to create a song of your own.

NOTE: If a chord progression is unique or very recognizable, change it. Substitute different chords, change the order of the chords, and change the length of time you hold the chords.

PART THREE

SONG STARTERS: MUSIC TRACKS

Music tracks accompany the vocal melody and lyrics of a song, adding energy, rhythmic feel, and harmony. Some music tracks are complex, filled with layers of instruments and beats. Others are as simple as a guitar strum. Both track styles can be effective; sometimes an "unplugged" version of a song can be just as powerful as one that's heavily produced.

At times, as you go through the Song Starters in the following sections, I'll suggest using ready-made resources like karaoke tracks, MIDI files, and music loops. If you use one of these in a recording, be sure to read any agreement you sign when you buy or license the music. It will spell out what you're allowed to do with your track. There may be limitations on the ways you can pitch or sell your recordings.

» START WITH A RHYTHM TRACK

The core of all contemporary hit songs is a steady rhythm. To start a song with a rhythm, all you really need is the ability to clap your hands or tap your feet to a regular, even beat. It's one of those basic things humans have always done — clap hands, stomp feet. You can move on from the "hands-feet" option into drum loops, MIDI files, and music apps, but it's all built on basic human rhythms. So, let's start there.

GET DOWN TO BASICS

201

Most hit songs in the Dance and Pop/Dance genres are built on a steady, repeated bass drum beat. Choose a comfortable, medium pace and clap your hands or stomp your foot. Keep the beat going as you work on your melody or lyric. Imagine a roomful of people dancing to your song and create a melody to match. Use colorful images and action words in your lyric. Record your melody and lyrics while keeping the beat going with claps or foot stomps. *(Example: "Put Your Hands Up" – Kylie Minogue, "Stronger" – Kelly Clarkson, "Stayin' Alive" – Bee Gees)*

202

Tap your foot to a steady, medium beat — not too fast. You can use a metronome to help you keep the beat steady. (There are plenty of free online metronomes and apps.) Clap along to the beat. To make things a little more interesting, keep tapping your foot to the same beat, but try clapping twice as fast. (Clap on each beat and once in between each beat.) Many hit songs use this groove. Make up a melody of your own and sing it along as you tap and clap. Play with it until you find something you like. Record it and add a lyric. *(Examples: "With Or Without You" – U2, "Every Breath you Take" – The Police, or add a little swing, like "California Girls" – The Beach Boys)*

203

Tap your foot to a slow, steady beat. Clap three times on each beat. To hear a great song with this groove, listen to "I Only Have Eyes for You" by The Flamingos. Clap along with the piano part. This "triple feel" creates a cool, swaying feel. With a little change of feel, it becomes waltz time. Listen to "Breakaway" by Kelly Clarkson, "Daughters" by John Mayer, or "Take It to the Limit" by the Eagles. Then write a verse and chorus with a waltz feel.

204

Focus on the drum or percussion track of any successful song you like. Clap, tap, or stomp along with the rhythm. Then keep the rhythm going on your own without the song. Create an original verse lyric and melody. Add a chorus. When you have something you like, record it so you don't forget it.

205

Play a rhythmic strum on guitar, damping the strings so there's no audible chord, just rhythm. You can get inspiration from a hit song groove or use any strum you like. Let the energy of the strum suggest a mood or feeling. Sing a verse melody with or without lyrics. When you have a verse you like, add a chorus in a higher note range. Then find the chords that go with your melody. Record it. *(Strumming examples: "Hey Soul Sister" – Train, "You're Beautiful" – James Blunt)*

USE YOUR HEARTBEAT AND A METRONOME

Your resting heartbeat averages around 75 beats per minute. When music with a steady beat is played, your heartbeat tends to speed up or slow down to match the rhythm of the song. Faster rhythms increase your heart rate and make you feel energized. Slower rhythms make you feel more introspective or melancholy. Of course, the chords, melody, lyrics, and production of your song will define the mood more specifically, but you can begin to create a basic energy level with a steady beat.

You'll be using a metronome for these Song Starters. You can find free online metronomes on the internet.

206

Set the tempo on your metronome around 70 to 75 beats per minute, about the pace of the average resting heartbeat. This tempo lends itself to a thoughtful mood, mulling over the important things in life. As the metronome ticks, create a melody, chord, or lyric idea that expresses an introspective, "taking stock of life and love" attitude and record them. *(Example: "Beautiful" – Christina Aguilera)*

207 ✎

Set the metronome between 125 to 135 beats per minute. This is the tempo of many contemporary dance songs. It makes people want to get up and move. Create a rhythm to the metronome beat by tapping on a tabletop, clapping your hands, and/or stomping on the floor. Then come up with a melody or lyric idea that expresses the energy you feel. *(Examples: "Titanium" – David Guetta & Sia, "Summer" – Calvin Harris)*

208 ✎

Set the metronome tempo to faster (150+) or slower (-60) speeds and see what kinds of melodies and grooves these beats suggest. Start a lyric or melody at this tempo as you clap, tap, stomp, or pound out a rhythm to the metronome.

START WITH A DRUM TRACK

Starting with a basic drum track can suggest an energy level and rhythmic feel for your song. Is it going to be a driven, frenzied Punk/Rock song? Or an upbeat, quirky, fun song? Or maybe a sad bluesy ballad? Your melody, chords, and lyrics will define the genre and emotion more specifically, but a drum track can begin to suggest any one of these styles before you lay down your first music note or lyric line. Knowing where you're starting from can help you aim your song toward a single genre and emotional target.

209

Drumdrops.com sells solo drum tracks in a range of different styles, all available in complete song form, called Practice Tracks. Audition a few. Pick a couple you like and start writing. A nice bonus: when you're ready to record your song, you can buy a multi-track version of the same drum track for high quality custom mixing.

210

Listen to the drum loops available at DrumsOnDemand.com. The loops are arranged in song sections — intro, verse, chorus, and bridge — with variations. They're available in a range of file formats. If you have any brand of music sequencing software, there should be a format that works for you. Lay out a drum track in song form and use one of the chord progressions in this book. Note the energy or mood of the rhythm track and write your song accordingly.

211

Look for the drum version of a hit song. Karaoke-version.com has plenty of these drums-only tracks. Start your song by writing lyrics and melody or lay down a chord progression to the drum track, and then write the song.

HINT: You can let the hit song suggest your song's genre and general emotional direction, but be sure you don't use any of the melody or lyric of the original hit.

212 🍃

Check out DrumAndBassTracks.com. Like karaoke tracks, these are based on well-known hit songs, but only drums and bass have been recorded. You can buy drum and bass together or drums alone. (The website is a little funky looking, but the tracks are good.) Download your mp3 and create an original lyric and melody to the drums, or drum and bass parts.

213 🍃

MIDI has come a long way from the stiff, robotic drum tracks of years past. A good MIDI drum part can rock or swing your song. You can create, modify, and play MIDI tracks in any professional music sequencing program (DAW). You'll find good MIDI files for DAWs at Loop Loft (theLoopLoft. com). For a cheaper, simpler option, try one of the many stand-alone apps for computer, tablet, or smartphone. Just search for "MIDI players" in the app stores. For MIDI files that will work with most apps, check out GrooveMonkee.com. Choose a drum track, add a chord progression from this book, and then write your melody and lyric.

214 🍃

Create a drum track with the drum machine apps that are available for computer, tablet, or smartphone. Just search the app stores for "drum machine app." Choose a rhythm and write a song with the feel the rhythm suggests.

215

Do an internet search for "drum machine online." Explore the styles available. Choose a style that suggests an attitude or character and write a song. Try a Reggae, Funk, or Classic Rock style and see where it takes you.

» START WITH AN INSTRUMENTAL GROOVE

If you play guitar or keyboards, you can create a solid music track to write to. It can be a simple guitar strum or piano accompaniment, or you can incorporate drum loops, instrument samples, and layers of synthesizers and percussion. In this section, you'll create basic rhythm and chord tracks. I'll refer you to some hit songs for rhythm ideas. Be sure you only use the rhythmic groove. Avoid copying any identifiable riffs or instrumental parts.

NOTE: If you don't play an instrument, jump to the next section, "Start a Song with a Karaoke Track."

START WITH A PIANO OR GUITAR GROOVE

216

Listen to one of these two songs and learn the rhythm groove on piano or guitar. Make up your own chord progression or use one from the Chord Starters section of this book. Work up a lyric and melody suggested by the feel of the instrumental track.

- "Someone Like You" – Adele (piano)
- "Hey There Delilah" – Plain White T's (guitar)

217

Choose one of these songs and learn to play the rhythm groove on piano or guitar. Use the lyric, chord, and melody Song Starters to help you build a verse and chorus based on the rhythm.

- "Hey, Soul Sister" – Train (guitar or ukulele)
- "You're Beautiful" – James Blunt (guitar)
- "Fallin'" – Alicia Keys (piano)

218

Pick one of these songs and learn to play the rhythm. When you can play the rhythm comfortably, pick up the pace or slow it down to your own taste. Let the rhythm suggest an attitude or mood for your song. Is it thoughtful and energetic? Upbeat or sad? Happy or angry? What are some words that describe the mood? Start a lyric with those. Use a chord progression from the Chord Starters section.

- "Let It Be" – The Beatles (piano)
- "Somebody That I Used To Know" – Gotye (guitar)
- "Ho Hey" – The Lumineers (guitar)

219

Select one of these songs and learn to play the rhythmic feel. Change the chords as you work up a new lyric and melody.

- "When I Was Your Man" – Bruno Mars (piano)

- "Riptide" – Vance Joy (guitar)

- "Love Song" – Sara (piano)

- "Mrs. Robinson" – Simon & Garfunkel (guitar)

220

A groove can suggest a lyric message. These two songs have a Reggae rhythm. Learn to play this feel and create a new song around it. Try giving your lyric an upbeat message of love and togetherness.

- "I'm Yours" – Jason Mraz

- "One Love" – Bob Marley & the Wailers

221

Write a song in waltz time (3/4 or 6/8). Try using one of these rhythmic feels to launch your song. Use a chord progression from the Chord Starters section of this book and work up a lyric and melody.

- "Sweet Baby James" – James Taylor (guitar)

- "You And Me" – Lifehouse (guitar)

- "Piano Man" – Billy Joel (piano)

- "Open Arms" – Journey (piano)

222

Play an acoustic guitar or piano rhythm based on any song you like. (Check out the list below for a few suggestions.) Use a chord progression of your own, or choose one from the Chord Starters section. Record a simple instrumental track so you can focus on lyric and melody writing. Work up a verse and chorus to your recording.

- "Jar Of Hearts" – Christina Perri (piano)

- "Gone Away" – Lucy Schwartz (piano)

- "Stitches" – Jaclyn Davies (piano cover version)

- "Collide – Acoustic Version" – Howie Day (guitar)

- "Marry Me" – Train (guitar)

- "Sleeping By Myself" – Eddie Vedder (ukulele)

» START WITH A KARAOKE TRACK

Whether you play an instrument or not, karaoke tracks can provide inspiration and a strong music base on which to practice songwriting, especially "top-line" writing (writing lyrics and melody to a producer's track).

Look for karaoke tracks without backing vocals. You can find them for sale on iTunes and at Karaoke-version.com. A karaoke track that relies on a generic three- or four-chord progression is your best choice because the chord progression isn't likely to be copyrighted.

If you use a karaoke track, you'll need to record a new music track for your song before you can pitch it. The karaoke track belongs to the company or producer who made it. However, you may be able to pay for additional rights. Look for contact information on the website where you found the track or use the "Get Info" command for the track in iTunes and ask the owners for the permissions you need.

Be sure you avoid using *any identifiable instrumental hooks or riffs, any unique chord progressions, or any part of the arrangement of the hit song.* If you're not sure whether your work is totally original, change any element that worries you, or *use the track for writing practice only.*

223

Choose a karaoke track from a hit song you know well. Listen to it and identify where the song sections begin. Where do the verses start? Where does each chorus come in? If there are pre-choruses or a bridge section, make a note of the starting points. If you need to, refer to the hit song until you find the sections. Create an original melody that fits the same song structure. If your melody sounds too much like the hit song melody, change the pitches and lengths of the notes. Play with it until you have something that's all your own. Add a few lyric lines in the verse and chorus. Make sure your lyric doesn't use any of the hit song lyric.

224

Select a karaoke track from a song you *don't* know. Identify the song sections. Notice where there is an increase or decrease in the energy of the track, where instruments are added or subtracted. Start a chorus when the energy reaches a peak. Start a verse when it decreases, or shortly afterwards. See if you can fit verse and chorus ideas into the track.

225

While listening to a karaoke track, write a list of images, feelings, and ideas that the track suggests to you. Start building a lyric around your word list as you listen to the track. For more lyric ideas, see the Lyric Starters section of this book.

226

Listen to a karaoke track and identify the point where you want to start a verse. Let the track suggest a mood or situation. Start a verse by singing a lyric line or humming a melody that expresses the mood or introduces a situation. If you like it, keep going.

227

Listen to a karaoke track and identify the point where you want to start your chorus. Create a song title. (See the Song Starters in "Start with a Title" for ideas.) Sing your title at the beginning of the chorus section. If you like what you hear, keep going.

228

Look for a karaoke track with a pre-chorus section between the verse and chorus. You should hear a difference in the arrangement — the addition of more instruments or a change in energy level though not as great as the chorus. Fill in that section as you work on your song.

229

Choose a karaoke track and imagine it being used as underscore in a scene in a movie or TV show. What's going on in the scene? What are the characters feeling? Imagine you're one of the characters. Sing what you think the character would say. Keep singing until you create something you like, and then build on it.

» START WITH A MUSIC APP OR WEBSITE

You can buy or create backing tracks to write to that are completely original (not based on existing hit songs like karaoke tracks). There are several ways to do this.

- Use music sequencing software or apps to make your own.

- Make backing tracks online and download as mp3s.

- Buy them pre-made as digital downloads or on CD.

Be sure to read any agreement you sign when you buy or license the tracks. It may limit what you can do with them.

230

Create a quick track online. Ujam.com and JamStudio.com are two websites where you can create a track by choosing the chords and instruments you want to use right on the website. Take a look at these websites and explore what's available. Rough out a few melody and lyric ideas. JamStudio requires a monthly fee if you want to save and download your work.

231

Play with an app on your smartphone or tablet. Guitarism and ChordBot are two apps that will let you input a chord progression and create a track. You can use the chord progressions in this book to launch yourself right into a song.

232

If you have an inexpensive music software program like Garageband or Acid Music Studio, or if you have a more expensive one like Logic, Pro Tools, Cubase, or Digital Performer, check out song "construction kits" at BigFishAudio.com and DrumsOnDemand.com. Change, mute, remix, or rearrange the instrumentation to suit your taste. Then create an original song to the track.

233

Take a look at Band In a Box (PGmusic.com). This software can create an original music track for you, and then write a melody based on your chord progression. The results sound a bit predictable, but it's a fun place to start. Make music changes to your taste and try a few lyric ideas. There's a free demo version.

234

Check out My Co-Writer at DrumsOnDemand.com or JustAddVocals.com. You'll find original instrumental tracks in various styles laid out in song form. Listen to a few of the tracks. If one or more of them suggests a song idea, continue working online or go ahead and purchase. (Stick with the cheaper, non-exclusive version.)

» START WITH A MUSICAL MOOD

A good song gives the listener an emotional experience, so you might want to start your song by building a music track that creates mood and attitude. To do this, you'll build on both chords and rhythm. The Song Starters in "Start With a Rhythm Track" can show you easy ways to create drum and percussion grooves. For chord progressions, refer to the Chord Starters in Part Two.

235

To create a music track for a song with a positive, upbeat attitude, choose a steady beat or rhythm track, one that's energetic but not frenzied. Select a chord progression that features simple three-note chords and a major feel. (Although the chords don't all need to be major chords.) Write a melody that emphasizes the notes in the basic three-note chords that accompany it. *(Example: "Technicolor" – Tim Myers)*

236

Start with a music track for a sad song. Choose a steady beat or drum track that's on the slow side. Use a chord progression with a minor feel. (Try a progression that starts with a minor chord.) Use a mix of melody notes, some in the basic three-note chord with others that are outside the chord (the 2nd, 4th, 6th and major 7th) to add an ambivalent or thoughtful feel. *(Examples: "Almost Lover" – A Fine Frenzy, "Walking On a Dream" – Empire of the Sun)*

237

Create a music track for an aggressive Rock song. Choose a rockin' drum loop at a fast pace (150 BPM or higher). Starting on or emphasizing minor chords is a good idea for this style, but not necessary. Try a mix of melody notes that are in the basic three-note chord with emphasis on notes that are between and around the notes of the chord to add some dissonance. *(Example: "The Pretender" – Foo Fighters)*

238

Create a music track for a quirky relationship song based on a piano groove that bounces along under a simple chord progression. Melody phrases that start on a variety of unpredictable beats and plenty of syncopation in the chorus melody throw the listener off balance, creating lots of surprises. *(Examples: "Love Song" – Sara Bareilles, "Girls Chase Boys" – Ingrid Michaelson)*

239

Watch a commercial on television and create a song for it. Express the attitude of the people or situation in the ad in your musical rhythm and chords.

STUDY HIT SONG ARRANGEMENTS FOR IDEAS

Look for inspiration and ideas for chords and rhythm in successful songs that express the attitude you're looking for. Here are a few to get you started.

240

Try a rhythm groove with swagger. A guitar strum like the one in "You're So Vain" by Carly Simon speaks volumes. Try that groove with a Rock-style melody and confident lyric.

241

Get your motor running with a chunky electric guitar groove like the one in "Born to Be Wild" by Steppenwolf. A rebellious lyric and a melody that hits a few bluesy notes will add the extra edge that completes the attitude.

242

Who wouldn't want to work on their tan while sipping umbrella drinks as they listen to the laid-back groove of a song like "Margaritaville" by Jimmy Buffett? Aim for a medium tempo (not too slow) and be sure to add a little sway to the guitar strum or piano track. Keep the chords and melody simple. Give listeners plenty of attractive, tactile imagery, like Buffett's "sponge cake," "sun bake," and "covered in oil."

243

The sweet innocence of Meiko's "Reasons to Love You" is created by a straightforward guitar rhythm, a simple chord progression, and a melody that sticks to the basic three-note chords that support it. Try something like that.

244

Ingrid Michaelson's "Be OK" evokes a sense of quirkiness and off-kilter energy by emphasizing the upbeats in the guitar part while featuring the strong beats in the vocal melody. A fast (but not frenzied) tempo adds energy and momentum. Create a guitar or piano part and a melody like that one.

245

Create some sparks with an uptempo, driving guitar strum like the one in Colbie Caillat's "Brighter Than the Sun." Add some organic percussion — handclaps and finger snaps — to keep things light and bright. Deliver a smile with a melody that features plenty of interval jumps, a mix of long and short phrases, and unusual line starts. You'll have a song that'll energize listeners, for sure.

PART FOUR

SONG STARTERS: MELODY

Many songwriters start a song with a lyric idea or write lyrics and melody together. But melodies can be a creative springboard on their own. Without a lyric, a melody is more fluid and adaptable. You can play with note rhythms, note pitches, and phrase lengths without having to worry about whether or not your new melody ideas will fit your lyric. Creating a melody first is a great way to get comfortable with writing and rewriting the most emotional and memorable element of your song.

One important thing to keep in mind as you write: vocal melodies are limited by the range of the human voice. If you're writing your melody on a keyboard, it's easy to forget that most humans, including many established recording artists, don't have a range greater than an octave and a half. So, even if you don't think you're a very good singer, try to stick to the notes you can sing yourself. Use nonsense syllables (la-la-la or da-da-da) as you write. Your melody will end up being much more singer-friendly.

» START WITH A MELODY PHRASE

A memorable melody often starts with a simple musical phrase. The following Song Starters will help you create several different melody phrases. Some might work together in the same song, or each one might turn into a different song. It's a good idea to record your melody ideas as you go. A good melody idea can easily slip away if you don't.

As you do these Song Starters, use a metronome, a basic drum loop, or tap your foot to keep time. It's not necessary, but it can make it easier to slip your melody phrases into a rhythm track later on.

246

Sing four notes. Make all of them the same length. (Try two beats each.) Change the note pitches. For example, try descending from high notes to low ones, or jump from a low note to a high one. When you find something that sounds like the first line of a song melody, repeat it, singing with a little more emotional energy. What does it make you feel? Sing a few words the melody suggests. Stop there or keep working on it.

247

Start a new melody with five notes. Use the note rhythm: short, short, long, long, long. An example of this note rhythm is the opening line of "Every Breath You Take" by The Police. Of course you can't use that melody; it's copyrighted. Instead, change the pitches of the notes. Try a series of rising notes or add a jump from high to low.

Repeat your melody line. Add emotional energy and try a few words with it. If you like it, keep working.

248

Sing six notes. Stretch out the first three notes and speed up the next three (long, long, long, short, short, short). Sing it a few times, changing the note lengths and pitches until you find something you like. Add or subtract notes to improve your melody. You can also change the rhythm of the notes. You might give it a Reggae or Latin feel. Slow it down and turn it into a ballad. Speed it up and make it a Punk/Rock song.

249

Use the Lyric Starters to create a few lyric phrases. Try them out with any of the melody phrases you've written. Add chords and record your rough ideas.

250

Sing the first line of "Twinkle Twinkle, Little Star" (seven notes). Drop out the lyric and use nonsense syllables (la-la or da-da). Change some or all of the note pitches. Change some or all of the note lengths. Pretty soon you should have a melody that doesn't sound anything like "Twinkle Twinkle, Little Star." If you like your melody idea, record it and add a lyric and chords.

251 ✎

Write a melody phrase with a pause in the middle and a mix of long and short notes. Listen to the chorus of John Legend's "All Of Me" to hear this idea. To avoid copying Legend's song melody, start with a short note followed by two long ones (short, long, long). Then repeat, changing the note pitches.

252 ✎

Start your melody with a series of short, repeated phrases. You can hear this pattern at the start of the chorus of "Smile" by Uncle Kracker. Sing a melody like his, but play with the rhythm and pitches of the notes until you have a new, original melody.

253 ✎

Choose any hit song you like and change the melody by varying the long and short note rhythms and the note pitches. Add your own chords.

254 ✎

Go through some of the melodies you've written. Repeat a line while varying some of the notes or lengthening the phrase with added notes. Then add chords and a few lyric ideas. If you like it, keep working on it.

» START WITH A MELODY & BEAT

The underlying propulsive rhythmic feel of today's hit songs — the groove — is a big part of a song's appeal. The groove can make you bob your head or leap up and dance. It sets the shuffling, swaying, jerky, or smooth feel of a music track. In turn, the groove affects the melody style and the way it is phrased. So, I recommend writing your melodies to a groove. Try using a percussion or drum loop, a drum app or MIDI file, or a pre-recorded drum track to create a groove and write to that. (See "Start With a Rhythm Track" for resources.) If you don't have access to a rhythm track, just clap to a steady beat or use a free online metronome.

255

Choose a rhythm loop or clap at a steady, medium pace (around 80 to 90 beats per minute). Count to four, one number on each beat. Sing each number on a beat. Change the pitches of the notes until you find a melody you like. Write a lyric phrase of four words or four syllables. Sing a word or syllable on each beat instead of a number. *(Song example: the chorus of "I'm Yours" by Jason Mraz)*

256

Choose a rhythm loop with a steady, medium pace. Count to four, one number on each beat as you did before, but add the word "and" between each beat: "1 and 2 and 3 and 4 and." Using nonsense syllables, sing a note on every beat and every "and." Play with it until you find a melody you like, and then record it. *(Example: the verse of "I'm Yours" by Jason Mraz is close to this idea.)*

257

Play a rhythm loop or clap at a steady, medium pace. Using nonsense syllables, sing some notes on the beat and some in the spaces between (on the "and"). Mix things up. Get creative. Leave as much space or fill in as many beats as you want. If you come up with a melody you like, record it. Add a lyric if desired.

258

Select a rhythm loop or clap at a steady, medium pace as you count to four silently. Using nonsense syllables, start singing a melody phrase on the second beat of each group of four. Practice this until you feel comfortable, and then explore a few ideas. Sing a mix of long and short notes. Play with the lengths of some of the phrases. Just be sure you start all of the lines on Beat 2. Add lyrics and chords if desired. Remember to change chords on the first beat of the bar, *not* when you start singing on Beat 2.

259

Choose a rhythm loop or clap at a steady, medium pace. Count to four silently. Start singing a melody phrase on the third or fourth beat of each group of four. Practice until you feel comfortable then start playing with it. Lengthen or shorten lines. Sing a mix of long and short notes. Just be sure to start your phrases on Beat 3 or Beat 4. If you find a melody you like, record it. Add chords and a lyric.

260

Pick an uptempo rhythm loop, something faster than you've been using. Feel the difference in energy level. Sing a melody that uses a mix of long and short notes. Try different patterns of notes. When you find a pattern of notes you like, repeat it. Then move on to a different pattern.

261

Choose a rhythm loop or clap at a steady, uptempo pace. Sing a melody phrase, and then repeat it starting on a different beat. Then sing it again starting on another beat. Use these repeated phrases to start a verse melody.

262

Choose any tempo and play a rhythm loop or clap at a steady pace. Using nonsense syllables, sing a melody that starts on an upbeat (the "and" after any beat). Try starting all your phrases on upbeats. Play with using long and short notes in different patterns. If you come up with a melody you like, record it and add chords and lyrics.

263 ♪

Listen to a hit song you like and count along with the underlying, steady beat. Notice where the melody phrases start in the hit song melody. Play a rhythm loop or clap an even, steady beat and sing a series of melody phrases starting on the same beats as the hit song. If your melody sounds too similar to the hit song, change the note pitches and lengths of the notes until it sounds different.

264 ♪

Try writing a melody to a lyric now. Use one of the Lyric Starters to create a lyric line. Choose the pace that you think expresses the feel of the lyric and keep a steady beat. Write a melody phrase to fit the lyric. If you like it, keep working on it. You can continue to write the lyric first, lyric and melody together, or melody first.

» START WITH A MELODY PATTERN

Today's hit songs feature melodies with plenty of unexpected twists and rhythms in them, few pauses where we expect them, and a variety of line lengths and phrase starts. These melodies can be quite complicated, yet listeners find them instantly catchy and memorable. The secret: Every verse and chorus features a very clear *pattern* of melody repetition and variation. Repetition makes the melody easy to remember, while variation keeps it interesting. I've included several of the most popular patterns right here for you to use.

In the following patterns, fill in Line 1 with one of the melodies you created in "Start With a Melody Phrase," or write a new melody phrase. Develop a complete song section by following the pattern line by line. If you'd like to hear an example of the melody pattern, listen to the reference song. I gave some suggestions for places to repeat or vary your lyrics in the pattern when you're ready to write them.

265

Pattern 1 *(Example: the chorus of "Highway Don't Care" – Tim McGraw)*

- Line 1: Your melody line (and lyric).

- Line 2: Repeat Line 1 melody (with lyric variation).

- Line 3: Repeat Line 1 melody and extend the length with an added phrase.

- Repeat all three lines for a complete song section.

266 ✎

Pattern 2 *(Example: the chorus of "Gone, Gone, Gone" – Phillip Phillips)*

- Line 1: Your melody line (and lyric).

- Line 2: Different melody line (new lyric).

- Line 3: Repeat Line 1 melody (with another new lyric).

- Line 4: Repeat Line 2 and extend length to wrap up as needed new lyric).

267 ✎

Pattern 3 *(Example: the verse of "Firework" – Katy Perry)*

- Line 1: Your melody line (and lyric).

- Line 2: Repeat Line 1 melody (new lyric).

- Line 3: Same note rhythm as Line 1 with different note pitches (new lyric).

- Line 4: Repeat Line 1 with a different note ending (new lyric).

The following melody patterns are a little more complex. Nothing needs to be perfect. Just use these for raw material, ideas to get your song started.

268

Pattern 4 *(Example: the verse of "Stand By You" – Rachel Platten)*

- Line 1: Your melody line (and lyric).
- Line 2: Same note rhythm as Line 1 but vary the end (new lyric).
- Line 3: A new melody line, longer than Line 1 and 2.
- Line 4: Similar to Line 1 but shorter (new lyric).

269

Pattern 5 *(Example: the verse of "Apologize" – OneRepublic)*

- Line 1: Your melody line (and lyric).
- Line 2: Repeat Line 1 melody (new lyric).
- Line 3: Repeat Line 1 melody rhythm with new note pitches.
- Line 4: Repeat Line 3 melody.

270

Pattern 6 *(Example: the chorus of "Hold Back The River" – James Bay)*

- Line 1: Your melody line (and lyric).
- Line 2: Repeat the first part of Line 1, and then change melody.
- Line 3: Repeat Line 1 melody (new lyric).
- Line 4: Repeat the first part of Line 1, and then change melody.

271

Pattern 7 *(Example: the chorus of "I Drive Your Truck" – Lee Brice)*

- Line 1: Your melody line (and lyric).

- Line 2: Repeat the first part of Line 1, and then change melody (new lyric).

- Line 3: A short melody phrase, repeated three or four times (new lyric).

- Line 4: A short to medium length melody line to wrap up.

272

Listen to some of your favorite hit songs. Identify the melody and lyric patterns in the chorus. Choose one of the songs and use the melody and lyric pattern to write a chorus of your own.

» START WITH THE MELODY OF SPEECH

When we speak, we express not only thoughts and ideas but also layers of emotional meaning. For instance, someone might say, "That's great." But how do we know if the speaker genuinely means it or is being sarcastic? How enthusiastic are they, a little or a lot? We interpret the emotion in that phrase by listening to the melody of speech. If the speaker's voice is pitched a little higher than normal, if the word "great" is emphasized with volume, if the rhythm of the words is fast-paced and energetic, then we feel the speaker is genuinely enthusiastic. But if the line is delivered in a low note range, the words are dragged out, the pitch descends, and there's little change in volume, then we interpret that as sarcasm. And we'd be right.

Every time we talk, in a sense, we sing. We use volume, pitch, and rhythm to make our words more expressive. The more emotion we're feeling, the more these musical elements are emphasized. Using the melody of speech as the basis for a song melody is a good way to ensure that the emotional meaning you want to convey is captured and communicated.

273

Picture yourself in a great mood. Everything is going right for you and good things are coming your way. Choose one of these lines and say it out loud with plenty of upbeat emotion. Repeat it three or four times. As you do, notice the pitch and rhythm of the words. Exaggerate the pitches until they become melody notes. Work with the rhythm as you tap or clap a medium to uptempo beat. When you have something you like, make it the first line of a verse.

- "It's a great day to be living."

- "I'm gonna feel like this forever."

- "I woke up this morning in a sunshine world."

274

Imagine yourself feeling sad. Choose one of these lines and say it with genuine feeling. Repeat it as needed and notice the pitch and rhythm of the words. Exaggerate the pitches until they become melody notes. Work with the rhythm as you tap or clap a steady, slow to medium beat. If you find something you like, make it the first line of a verse.

- "I should've seen the writing on the wall."

- "I reached for a dream but it slipped through my hands."

- "In a place where my voice is just an echo in the night."

275

Imagine you're feeling angry. Choose one of these lines and say it with genuine feeling. Repeat it with plenty of emotion and notice the pitch and rhythm of the words. Exaggerate the pitches until they become melody notes. Explore rhythm ideas as you tap or clap a steady beat at a pace that feels right to you. When you have something you like, adjust the lyric and melody as needed and make it the first line of a chorus.

- "Never gonna say okay to that!"

- "Smash it into pieces."

- "No more messing around."

- "You gotta pay the price!"

- "I see through all your lies."

276

When we ask a question or we're uncertain, our voices tend to rise at the end of the line. Choose one of these questions and repeat it with genuine feeling. Find a melody in the lines as you clap a steady beat. When you've got something you like, adjust the lyric and melody and make it the first line of a verse.

- "Are we running out of time?"

- "Do you really love him/her?"

- "Can we make this world a better place?"

- "How will I know if you're telling me the truth?"

277

Falling in love is something we've all felt. Choose one of the following lines and say it with real emotion. Repeat it until you can hear the pitch and rhythm of the line. Exaggerate them until you hear a melody as you clap a steady beat. Add chords and adjust the lyric and melody as needed. Make it the first line of a chorus.

- "I never knew what love was all about... till now."

- "My love is wide as the ocean and deep as the sky."

- "Let me be your lover and we'll live and love forever."

278

Determination and strength have been the subjects of several hit songs. Use this line: "I'm strong enough to make it on my own," or write a line of your own. Repeat it with confidence and strength until you can hear the pitch and rhythm of the words. Find the chords and strum or play a rhythm that underscores that feeling.

279

Listen to Carly Simon's "You're So Vain" or CeeLo Green's "Forget You." Notice how the title line and others are delivered in a derisive tone as a "put down." Try using one of the following lyric lines in a song and create a chorus melody with that put-down tone.

- "You don't know what you're talkin' about."

- "I can do so much better than that."

- "You won't even know I'm gone."

- "There's nothin' goin' on here."

280

Picture yourself at the hottest nightclub in town. The music is slammin', the beautiful people are dancing, and the crowd is crammed close together. As the rhythm pounds and the lights swirl, suddenly you find yourself dancing with the sexiest guy or girl you've ever seen. What do you say? How do you say it? Look for the melody in the words, and then sing it like you mean it! Add a solid four-on-the-floor rhythm track and get busy.

281

Watch a scene in a movie or TV show, one with a lot of emotion. Listen for dialogue lines that are delivered with feeling and notice the pitch, rhythm, and emphasis. Exaggerate those elements and turn the line into a melody and lyric. Add chords and a beat.

» START WITH THE MELODY OF EMOTION

If you're writing a song or instrumental cue for the Film & Television market, you'll be asked to evoke a particular mood or emotion with your melody. ("We need a song for a romantic, falling-in-love scene!" "We need a cute, quirky kids' song with loads of energy for a scene where a children's party spins out of control.")

Melody is the gateway to emotion. While lyrics can tell us who exactly is feeling that emotion and what's causing it, it's up to the music to evoke those waves of joy or sadness, fighting spirit or resignation, mellow moments, or dance mania.

Although emotional expression in melody can be a subjective thing, there are some tricks you can use that will generally evoke the mood you want. I've included suggestions with each Song Starter.

Keep in mind while you work on these that a piece of music doesn't have to be complicated or difficult to be expressive. It can be as simple as a solo vocal melody line. Just think about the emotional power of a single voice singing "Amazing Grace" or a bunch of kids singing "Boom, Boom! Ain't It Great To Be Crazy." Put some of *that* in your melody and sing it!

Here we go...

282

Imagine yourself in a peaceful, calm place. Play or sing a melody that expresses this sense of peace and calm.

HINT: Keep the volume soft. Use some note repetition. Don't use any sudden, large interval jumps. If desired, add chords that support the feeling. Use the ideas in Part Four "Start With a Melody Pattern" to develop your phrase into a verse or chorus. *(Example: "Peaceful Easy Feeling" – Eagles)*

283

Write a melody for a cartoon in which two silly characters fall in love and go on a honeymoon.

HINT: Try something at a medium to fast pace. Give your melody plenty of unexpected jumps and twists. Try singing nonsense syllables to add to the fun. Consider singing your melody then playing a verse on kazoo or slide whistle. Add chords if desired. *(Example: "The Birds and the Bees" – Patrick and Eugene)*

284

Imagine a character who is angry and aggressive. Play or sing a melody that conveys anger and aggression.

HINT: Try tapping your foot or even stomping your heel at a steady, medium tempo to get into the mood. Use plenty of short repetitive notes.

An interval jump upward can give you a chance to "attack" a note. As you work on your melody, add chords and rhythm that support the feel. Use the ideas in "Start With a Melody Pattern" to develop your phrase into a verse or chorus. *(Example: "The Pretender" – Foo Fighters)*

285 ✐

Imagine someone who is excited and elated. Something good is happening or about to happen. Play or sing a melody that you feel expresses excitement, happiness, or anticipation.

HINT: Try a medium to fast tempo. Give the melody plenty of bounce by jumping between notes that are not next to each other. Use a syncopated rhythm in the melody and rising pitches. *(Examples: "Walking On Sunshine" – Katrina and the Waves, "Technicolor" – Tim Myers)*

286 ✐

Write a melody for a scene in which someone has lost the person they love. Put yourself in that situation and try to imagine a melody that expresses yearning as well as memories of time spent together.

HINT: Try a slow to medium ballad style rhythm. Consider a melody with some upward leaps and soaring lines. Give it some wings! *(Example: "My Heart Will Go On" – Celine Dion)*

287

Imagine yourself feeling proud and self-assured. There's a swagger in your step and in the music that expresses your confidence. Go ahead and boast. Strut around the room. Now, write a melody with that same swaggering feel. Add chords and rhythm if desired. *(Example: "We Are the Champions" – Queen)*

For more ideas on starting your song with attitude and mood, see "Start With a Musical Mood" in Part Three.

PART FIVE

THE SONG STARTERS GRAB BAG

Loosen up your muse. Warm up your wordsmithing. Get your melody maker humming. Jump in anywhere on these pages and grab an idea. Try it out. See what happens. Work on it for a while to see where it takes you. It could be the best song you ever wrote or it could end up as scratch paper. But you'll never know if you don't try.

» LYRIC STARTERS GRAB BAG

288

Write a song about a rumor. Who told it? What was it about? How did it affect someone?

289

Write a song that asks a series of questions. *(Example: "What's Love Got to Do with It?" – Tina Turner)*

290

Look for a television commercial that uses a song. (There are a lot!) Write a song that could replace the song in the ad. Try to capture a similar energy and emotion in your song, but don't copy the ad song.

291

Watch a dance scene in a film like *Saturday Night Fever, Flashdance, Footloose, Dirty Dancing, Step Up, Singing in the Rain,* etc. Turn off the sound and write a song for the scene. You can also do this with dance competition TV shows. Just turn the sound off and write a new song for the couple to dance to.

292

Watch a children's cartoon show. Write a new theme song for it.

293

Write a song in which you are not prepared for the things that happen.

294

Write a song for your pet. If you don't have a pet, write one for any pet you ever had or a friend's pet. How do you feel about that animal? How does it feel about you? Try a song from the pet's point of view.

295

Listen to one of these songs, and then write a quirky, happy love song of your own.

- "Birdhouse In Your Soul" – They Might Be Giants
- "The Birds And The Bees" – Patrick and Eugene
- "5 Years Time" – Noah and the Whale

296

Write a song about your favorite holiday memory. Let listeners know why it's your favorite, who was there, and what happened.

297

Write a song about your worst holiday memory and what happened that ruined it for you.

298

Write a song about being an average, ordinary, regular person. You can make it a positive or a negative in your song.

299

Write a song about being different, being unique, or being an outsider. *(Examples: "Born to Run" – Bruce Springsteen, "Beautiful" – Christina Aguilera.)*

300

Write a song about the best advice you ever received, or the worst advice. Or both! It's up to you.

301

Write an opening lyric line and send it to another songwriter. Ask them to write the next line and send it back. Write the line that comes after that one and send it back again, etc. When you have a verse and chorus lyric roughed out, write a melody the same way.

302

Write a song about some of the differences between women and men.

303

Write a song without using the word "I."

304

Write a song about a group of people. *(Example: "The 'In' Crowd" – Dobie Gray.)*

305

Write a song in which your inner child talks to you.

306

Write a song about writing songs.

307

Write a song in a place where you don't usually write. Get out of your bedroom or your studio. Write outdoors. Write in a tree. Write at a bus stop or a restaurant. Be inspired by whatever is in your surroundings.

308

Base your song on a fortune cookie saying. Use the saying to suggest a theme, a situation, or an actual lyric line. You can buy a bag of fortune cookies at the market, or go out to dinner at a Chinese restaurant, or use one of these to get your song started.

- A chance meeting brings happiness.

- You learn from your mistakes.

- Meeting a challenge well builds strength.

- Love can last a lifetime, but you must want it to.

- Value others and they will see your worth.

- The greatest risk is not taking a risk.

- You are the source of your own happiness.

- Expect news from a stranger.

309

Is there something you regret doing or not doing? Write a song about it.

310

Write a song in which you do impossible things. Make the things more and more impossible as the song goes along. *(Example: "Gone, Gone, Gone" – Phillip Phillips)*

311

Listen to early Elvis Presley hits, like "Hound Dog," "Heartbreak Hotel," and "Jailhouse Rock." Write a song in that style. Make it good enough to pitch to a young Elvis.

312

Write a love song that does not use the word love.

313

Write about someone's hands. What do the hands say about that person?

314

Base your song on a fairytale, folktale, or myth. You can refer directly to the story, using character names, or follow the plot line using contemporary characters and details. *(Example: "Stealing Cinderella" – Chuck Wicks)*

Here are a few stories with theme ideas:

- Cinderella – Transformed by love from misery to happiness.
- Sleeping Beauty – Awakened to love with a kiss.
- Beauty and the Beast – Loving someone's true nature, even if others can't see it.

- Echo and Narcissus – In love with someone who only loves him or herself.

- Chicken Little – A friend who always expects the worst.

- King Midas – Success in everything but love.

315 ✑

Base your song on a storyline that's a proven winner. Use the story and characters as inspiration. Look for the underlying theme and build on it. *(Example: "Love Story" – Taylor Swift)*

- Romeo and Juliette – A love story, what else?

- The Three Musketeers – Friends who stick together.

- Little Women – The importance of family ties.

Start a song idea with a comparison. Write a lyric in which you...

316 ✑

Compare love to a river, a fire, or a warm coat.

317 ✑

Compare a broken heart to a desert, a rainstorm, or a car crash.

318

Compare falling in love to diving into water, a carnival ride, or dreaming.

319

Compare a feeling of achievement to a map, a sunset, or a victory dance.

320

Compare family ties to a tangle of string or a garden.

321

Compare a feeling of surprise with an earthquake or an electric shock. Build a song on five things…

322

Make a list of FIVE things that are red. Use them all in a song.

323

Make a list of FIVE things you associate with winter. Write a song with all of those words in it. Use one in the title.

324

List FIVE things you could buy if you were rich. Write a song that explains why you would buy them, or why you wouldn't.

325

List FIVE things a trustworthy person does or doesn't do. Using all five, write a song in which you try to convince someone they should trust you, or not.

326

List FIVE things you would say to someone you have a crush on. Write a song and use all five.

327

Think of FIVE places you'd like to go with someone you love. Put them all in a song.

328

Think of FIVE reasons you like being home. Use all of them in a song. Try to make the listener see what you see and feel what you feel about home.

329

Write down FIVE things you want people to remember about you after you're gone. Use the one that's most important to you in your chorus lyric.

» CHORD STARTERS GRAB BAG

330 ✎

Write a song with only one chord. *(Examples: "Chain of Fools" – Aretha Franklin, "Coconut" – Harry Nilsson)*

331 ✎

Write a song with two chords. *(Examples: "Paperback Writer" – The Beatles, "A Horse With No Name" – America)*

332 ✎

Write a song using only major chords. *(Examples: "Knockin' On Heaven's Door" – Bob Dylan, "The Tide Is High" – Blondie)*

333 ✎

Write a verse and chorus, starting one section with a major chord and the other section with a minor chord. *(Example: "Norwegian Wood" – The Beatles)*

334 ✎

Use the chords of a hit song and write a completely new melody and lyric to it.

335

Look through the Chord Starters section in this book. Choose a progression and play it in reverse, starting with the last chord. Repeat as needed to write a song.

336

Choose a progression from the Chord Starters section. Write a song in waltz time (3/4). Hold each chord for two bars. For an interesting effect, start your melody lines halfway through each two-bar phrase. *(Example: "Place to Be" – Nick Drake)*

337

Think of a melody as having a shape. Write a melody that looks like a straight line. *(Example: "One Note Samba" – Antonio Carlos Jobim)*

338

Write a melody in which the verse is in a comfortable, conversational note range. Sing the chorus using the same melody one octave higher.

Examples:

- "If I Were A Boy" – Beyoncé
- "Iris" – The Goo Goo Dolls
- "Piano Man" – Billy Joel

USE A MELODY CLICHÉ

Just as there are lyric clichés, there are also melody clichés. Nursery rhymes, folk tunes, and camp songs all have melodies so familiar and predictable, they have become clichés. But just like verbal clichés, you can make use of these to start a song. By changing, twisting, and varying the melody, you can create something unexpected and fun for the listener.

As you work with the following Song Starters, drop out the lyric of the well-known song and write a new lyric or sing nonsense syllables.

339

Use the first line of a nursery rhyme melody to start your song. Play with the rhythm and pitches of the notes until you create a new melody. Add chords and a rhythm track.

Songs to use:

- "Twinkle, Twinkle Little Star"
- "Mary Had a Little Lamb"
- "Old MacDonald Had a Farm"
- "A-Tisket, A-Tasket"

340

Find a drum track or MIDI file with a Rock, Pop, Reggae, or Blues feel. (See "Start with a Rhythm Track" for resources.) Sing a melody over it using one of these campfire song melodies or a public domain melody of your choice. Change the rhythm of the melody to suit the drum rhythm. Then change the note pitches until you have a new melody. When you find a melody you like, record it.

Songs to use:

- "Home On the Range"
- "Kumbaya"
- "The More We Get Together"
- "I've Been Working On The Railroad"

341

Do an internet search for "public domain songs." Choose one, add a rhythm track, change the chords, and adapt the melody to your taste. Write a new lyric to your new melody.

342

Choose one of the public domain folk or campfire songs mentioned in this section and sing it to a Bossa Nova beat. Change the melody pitches and note rhythms until it sounds more, well... bossa-ish. Then write a Bossa Nova song of your own.

Examples of the Bossa Nova beat:

- "The Girl From Ipanema" – João Gilberto, Astrud Gilberto, Stan Getz
- "Desafinado" – João Gilberto
- "Bim Bom" – Bebel Gilberto
- "Misty Roses" – Tim Hardin

343

Write a song with a traditional Blues-style melody.

Examples:

- "Statesboro Blues" – Taj Mahal
- "Bright Lights, Big City" – Jimmy Reed

PART SIX

REWRITING SONGS WITH SONG STARTERS

You can use Song Starters to give new life to an unfinished song or polish up one that's less-than-stellar. If you have a lyric that feels a little ho-hum, a verse melody that's not lighting your fire, a chord progression or rhythm track that isn't working, take a look at some of these ideas for rewriting them.

» LYRIC REWRITES

344

Replace any action word in your lyric with a different action word. Try a word that's more intense or unique. For example, you could replace "ran" with "slipped" or "skipped" or "slid."

345

Remove any references to specific places or names and replace them with descriptive words. How does this person walk, talk, or look at you? What does this place look like or sound like? Is it warm or cold? Is it noisy or quiet? Replace the proper name with one of those words. *(Example: "Ebony Eyes" – Bob Welch, "Sk8er Boi" – Avril Lavigne)*

346

Replace an object with what the object feels like when you touch it.

347

Replace an emotion with the physical feeling of that emotion. For example, "I love" might become "I fall," "I fly," or "I breathe."

348

Add another physical sense to your lyric. If you haven't used taste, hearing, or smell, add a reference to one of those. What does something in your lyric sound, smell, or taste like?

349

Make something in your song more human. ("That ring on your finger just told me you're taken." "My heart has got a mind of its own.")

350

Write something that's way too emotional. Record it and listen back to it a few times over the next day or two. If you're still not comfortable with it, reel it back in a little at a time.

351

Answer the following questions: What do I want this song to tell listeners? What do I want them to understand? Read your lyric and add anything that's missing. Remove anything that's confusing or doesn't say what you want.

» MELODY REWRITES

352

Listen to a hit song in the style you want to write in and use the pattern of long and short phrases in the verse or chorus to rewrite your melody. Make your lines as long or short as those in the hit song by adding or subtracting notes and words.

353

Add some space to one of your melody lines. Put a pause somewhere in the middle of a line.

354

Divide the last line of your verse melody into two or more short, repeated melody phrases. Try to keep your lyric unchanged. Just phrase it differently if needed.

355

Raise your chorus melody up a third. Or lower it.

356

Record your melody. Take a break and go do something else until you forget about it. Come back and listen. Make one change.

357

Start your chorus melody one or two beats earlier. Shorten the line before it if you need to.

358

Start your verse or chorus melody on the upbeats (the "and" between the beats). Continue emphasizing the upbeats throughout that section.

» CHORD REWRITES

359

If you are changing chords on Beat 1 of every bar, add a new chord on Beat 3. It can be a chord you're not using anywhere else, it can be a simple substitution, or it can be a chord you use a lot in the song.

360

Replace one of the major chords in your progression with a minor chord.

361

Change the last chord of your verse or the first chord of your chorus.

362

Add a single, repeated note that plays through your entire chord progression, making the chords more complex. *(Example: "Walking on a Dream" – Empire of the Sun)*

» RHYTHM TRACK REWRITES

363

Try singing your song slower or faster. Imagine you are "covering" your own song. Reinterpret it.

364

Listen to successful songs you like until you hear a rhythmic groove that appeals to you. Learn to play it using the chords to your song. Sing your song to the new groove.

365

If your rhythm is busy, empty it out. Play less, add space while keeping the same tempo. If the rhythm has a lot of space, fill it in with more strumming or fingerpicking while keeping the tempo the same.

PART SEVEN

WRITE A SONG IN FOUR STAGES

Every once in a while, you get a song that's a breeze to write, expresses exactly what you want to say, and gets just the reaction you want from listeners. When that happens, acknowledge your brilliance and go record it.

But more often, a song you think is finished really isn't. It doesn't have the emotional punch you'd hoped for. It isn't as memorable as it could be. Or listeners just don't seem to get it.

Most successful songs are the result of a creative process, something that takes place over time, in stages. It's important to use that time to explore the melodies and rhythms in your song, to push the lyric envelope, and seek out more memorable ways to express yourself. Too often songwriters jump over these in-between stages, forcing the song to be finished before it's ready.

The best thing about writing in stages is: *You can undo anything and go back to what you had before.* If something isn't working, then scrap it, or keep the ideas that work and push ahead. It's all fluid. It's a time for experimentation, a time to reach for the best work you can do. You will never know what your best sounds like until you risk finding out.

THE FIRST STAGE

<u>KEEP A RECORD OF YOUR FIRST IDEA:</u> If you know what you want to write about, sum it up in one or two sentences and write it down. List any lyric phrases, images, actions, examples, and related thoughts that occur to you in connection with your song idea. Record any melody, chord, or rhythm ideas that come to you in connection with your idea. No matter how raw it sounds, try to capture the feeling and energy you have in mind. Keep this recording so you can refer to it whenever you want to remind yourself of the original inspiration for the song.

START WITH A TITLE

There are many ways to start a song. There are 365 in this book and many more I haven't thought of, I'm sure. However, starting with a title has some advantages.

- A title can help you stay focused on a central theme or idea as you write.

- Your title is going to feature prominently in your chorus. Starting your song with a memorable line in that important spot is easier than looking for one later on.

- A title can provide raw material that will help you as you construct your verses and chorus.

If you don't have a title yet, take a look through the Lyric Starters in the "Start with a Title" section of this book. Use those to work up a few ideas and choose one to start with.

VISUALIZE YOUR SONG STRUCTURE

While it might seem odd to think about the structure of your whole song before you work on lyrics or melody, it can be useful to have a general outline in mind, like the sketch an artist makes before starting a painting. Give yourself a general outline to work with. If you're not happy with it later, you can change it.

Most radio hits are roughly based on this structure:

> VERSE 1 / CHORUS / VERSE 2 / CHORUS / BRIDGE / CHORUS

Song structures are flexible. You'll often hear an extra section, called a "pre-chorus," between the verse and chorus. Some songs have a bridge section after the second chorus; some don't. A song can end with a repeat of the full chorus or just a few lines. Some songs, especially those aimed at the Film & Television market, don't have a chorus at all. Each verse ends with the same line, called a "refrain line," which is repeated once or twice.

STAGE 1: LYRICS

You can start a song with a lyric alone, or lyrics and melody together. Whichever you choose, here are some tips for making your first lyric draft count. (If you're starting with the melody first, go to "STAGE 1: MUSIC" below.)

- **STEP 1) Keep your core idea or song title in front of you.** On a piece of paper, write one sentence that sums up the heart of your idea. It could be a phrase that describes the emotion or situation you want to write about. Or it could be your song title or opening line. If you don't have a concept in mind, use the suggestions in the Lyric Starters section of this book to help you find one. Write your idea or title in big letters and put it where you can see it, on the wall, on your desk, on the floor in front of you. It will keep your song focused and on track while you write.

- **STEP 2) Create raw material.** Make a list of phrases, images, action words, comparisons, and examples related to your core idea or song title. You'll be coming back to this list as you write. Think about the emotional feel of your song and include words and phrases that are associated with that emotion. If you're writing a sad song, you might add words like "alone," "winter," "empty," or "dark." What would you *compare* the feeling to? How does it *physically* affect you? What *images* does it suggest? For more ideas, read the Lyric Starters section "Start with an Emotion."

- **STEP 3) Make a list of questions.** Look at your core idea and write down a list of questions you might like to answer in your song, questions like: What does this mean? Why is it important to me? How do I feel about it? What have I learned from it? What are my hopes and fears around it? Your listeners will have questions, too: What is happening? Who is involved? What is the singer feeling and why?

Verse 1 – Lyric Tips

- **Get listeners involved.** Drop your listeners into the middle of the situation in the first verse. There's no need to start at the very beginning. ("I met you on a Monday…" Nope.) Tell them something interesting about what's going on or who's involved. Don't assume they'll stick around to find out more. Make them *want* to stay.

- **Use your raw material.** Use some of the raw material you created in Step 2 above. Is there an image, action, or example that would give listeners a sense of what's happening? An example might be: "Since you left, I'm living life in black and white." An image or feeling might be: "Never thought I'd get this close to heaven." Try to paint a vivid picture of the situation and the people in it.

- **Write it down.** Write out any phrases or lines on a piece of paper and label it "Verse 1." Remember these are just ideas. Don't worry about line length or rhyming. For now, a few phrases, images, and ideas will do.

Chorus 1 – Lyric Tips

- **Use your song title.** If you have a title for your song, use it as the first and/or last line of your chorus. Write it down below your verse ideas and label it "Chorus." If you don't have a title yet, look through the list of raw material phrases you created in Step 2 above and choose one that expresses the emotion or situation you want to communicate. Feature that phrase in your chorus for now. You can rework it later, if needed.

- **Fill out your chorus idea.** Drop in a phrase from your raw material list that expands on or explains your core idea. Tell listeners what your core idea feels like or what your title means. Say the most important thing you want listeners to know. Don't worry about rhyming. Just say what you need to say.

Verse 2 – Lyric Tip

- **Sketch out an idea.** Where will you take your listeners? Will you give them detail about what led up to the situation, or examples of what's happening now? Or do you want to go deeper into why this is important or what the singer wants to do about it? All of these will work. Write down your Verse 2 ideas after your first chorus and label it "Verse 2."

Chorus 2 – Lyric Tip

- **Copy your chorus lyric.** Copy the lyric ideas you have for your first chorus and write them down following your Verse 2 ideas. Label it "Chorus 2." You should begin to see your song structure taking shape.

> **_HOT TIP: Don't edit yourself as you write._** Just get your ideas and feelings down on paper roughly in song form. If you find you're writing a lot of clichés or you can't think of anything to say, imagine yourself in the situation you're writing about. What does it feel like? What is the most important thing you see? How does your body feel? What images, colors, or physical sensations does it make you think of? Add the answers to your raw material list and try a few in your verse or chorus lyrics until you have something that looks promising. If you don't like it, you can always change it.

STAGE 1: MUSIC

Your melody is going to determine the emotional feel of the song for listeners. So, this is a good time to revisit the core idea or theme of your song. Are you writing about lost love, finding happiness, celebrating a milestone? What's the underlying emotion? Look to your inspiration and creativity first. Put yourself in the mood and write what comes to you. Record any melody ideas that sound promising. Here are a few techniques for writing verse and chorus melodies that express an attitude or emotion.

- **STEP 1) Choose a tempo.** The underlying steady beat of a song, the *tempo,* can convey energy. A mid to upbeat pace lifts the listener's energy level. A slower pace can create an introspective, thoughtful feel. Choose the one you think best reflects your song's core idea and clap or tap your foot to a steady, even beat. You can use an online metronome, a click track, or a basic MIDI drum pattern to keep the tempo steady.

- **STEP 2) Choose a groove.** The rhythm *groove* adds attitude, character, or vibe to a song. If you've already started your lyric, you probably have a good idea of the attitude you want to express in your song. Read the section titled "Start with a Rhythm Track" for ideas on how to put together a simple rhythm track. If you prefer, you can just clap or tap your foot to the steady underlying beat and let the melody create the groove.

- **STEP 3) Set the emotional tone with chords.** As you play the steady beat or the groove of your song, try out a few major or minor chords. Which chords fit the mood better? Remember that a happy or upbeat feel doesn't mean you'll *only* use major chords. You might start and end on major chords, passing through a minor. The same goes for a chord progression with a minor feel. Starting on a minor chord can be enough to set the mood. Check out a few successful songs with the mood you want and notice how the chord progression supports the feeling. Or try some of the chord progressions in this book. (See Part Two.)

- **STEP 4) Express emotion in your melody.** If you're writing your melody without a lyric, use your core idea or the general mood you want to express as your guide. For example, an emphasis on descending melody lines tends to pull the emotion in a dark or sad direction; ascending lines tend to be uplifting. For more ideas, read "Start with the Melody of Emotion" in Part Four of this book.

- **STEP 5) Use the natural melody of speech.** If you've started your lyric, you can begin your melody by using the music that occurs naturally when you speak. Say your title or a few of your lyric phrases out loud. Use plenty of honest emotion and notice how the words rise and fall in pitch and volume as you say them. Choose the line you like best and repeat it a few times with as much emotion as you can. (The more emotion you use, the more melody you'll hear.) Exaggerate the rhythm and pitches of the words until you have the beginning of a melody. For more ideas on using the melody of speech, read "Start With the Melody of Speech" in Part Four of this book.)

- **STEP 6) Add contrast to your melody.** Your verse melody will generally be in a lower note range than the chorus. Save the highest melody notes for the chorus. A good rule of thumb: Keep your verse melody in a conversational range, one you might use when explaining something to someone. Think of your chorus melody as more emotionally expressive.

Record your STAGE 1 draft

Now is the time to put together a *very rough* idea of your song — chords, melody, and lyrics. You're just trying to get a general idea of the verse and chorus at this point. If you don't have a melody for a line, speak the lyrics or leave a blank space. You can fill it in later. If lyric lines are missing, just "la-la" your way through. Use your rhythm track, a click track, or metronome to keep a steady beat.

Start recording and start the metronome or rhythm track. Sing as much of the melody and lyric as you have for each section. If you're only writing lyrics, read them out loud into the recorder, or sing them to a hit song melody to get a feel for the flow.

Take a break. Then come back later to listen with fresh ears.

THE SECOND STAGE

By now you should have a general idea of your song's energy and emotional feel. You also have a list of lyric phrases (your raw material) with some of them sprinkled into your chorus and verse, plus ideas for your melody and chords. In Stage 2, you're going to flesh this out, developing the lyric and melody further.

LISTEN TO YOUR DRAFT

Play your recording to see if it's *generally* what you are aiming for. There will be stumbles and empty lines, but try to hear past those. Just see if you think your rough idea will eventually evoke the mood and energy you want.

- **STEP 1) Make a "to do" list.** As you listen, try to hear the song the way a listener would, someone who has never heard it before. Write down any new ideas and any lyric, melody, or chord changes you want to make. Make those changes before you do anything else.

- **STEP 2) Add to your raw material.** Now is a good time to revisit your raw material list. Add more images, examples, descriptions, and action words to your list. Try a few comparisons: "This love is like a runaway train" or "Angry words are like a knife, sharp and dangerous."

> **_HOT TIP:_** **_Chorus and verse lengths._** There's no rule regarding the length of the chorus or verse. Take the time you need to say what you want to say. If you feel that your verse is too long, split it into two verses, or a verse and a pre-chorus. If you're still not sure, listen to a few successful songs you like and see if your verse and chorus lengths fall somewhere close to those.

STAGE 2: LYRICS

Verse 1 – Lyric Tips

- **Write a strong opening line.** It's important to catch the listener's attention with your very first line. Try an intriguing statement about the situation, a vivid image, a question, or comparison. You'll find more ideas in "Start With a Title" in Part One. These tricks work just as well for opening lyric lines.

- **Answer a question.** Let your listeners know what's happening as the song unfolds. Your first verse is a good place to start. Choose a question and answer it. Try one of these: What's happening? Who is involved? What is the singer feeling? Your answer can be as poetic or straightforward as you want.

- **Look for possible rhymes.** Give yourself plenty of choices by using "near rhymes" — rhymes in which the vowel sound is the same but not the consonants. If nothing occurs to you, move on. You'll work more on this later.

Chorus – Lyric Tips

The chorus is the emotional heart of your song. It's the purest expression of what the singer is feeling, while the verses give the listener information about the situation, the people involved, or the singer's thoughts. Try to avoid getting into explanations in the chorus. Save those for the verses. Focus on feelings instead.

- **Say it differently.** If you started your chorus with your title or another strong phrase, consider saying it in a different way in the second line. Imagine finishing the sentence: "What this really means is..."

- **Express the emotion.** In the middle lines of the chorus, tell listeners how the singer feels or why this is important to him or her. Use an image, physical sensation (touch, taste, hearing), or action words to convey the way the emotion feels. Finish the phrase, "I *need* to say this because..."

- **Give your chorus a payoff.** The last line of the chorus is sometimes called the "payoff" line. Give your listeners a strong emotional phrase or final thought to take away with them. Create a sense of completion. This can often involve the title as part of a longer line.

- **Check for rhymes.** Small changes in wording or a different way to say something can create a rhyme, but don't change the meaning of a line to accommodate a rhyme. Later on, you'll have a chance to work on rhymes in more depth.

STAGE 2: MUSIC

Verse 1 – Melody Tips

- **Keep it conversational.** Write your verse melody in a comfortable vocal range, something close to your normal speaking voice. If you have an opening lyric, say it a few times in a normal tone of voice. Notice where the pauses are, the pace of the words, and the way the line ends. Try copying that in a melody. Play with note pitches or rhythms until you have a melody phrase you like. Use that as the first line of your verse melody.

- **Use a melody pattern.** Look through the suggestions in "Start with a Melody Pattern" in Part Four, or listen to the verses of successful songs for line lengths and patterns of repetition. Try a similar pattern in your verse.

- **Tweak it.** Adjust your lyric lines to fit your melody or your melody to fit your lyric. Don't be afraid to extend a line with extra notes and words, even if it runs into the next one. Or you can break a line into short, repeated phrases. Play with a few different ideas until you find something you like. Record your idea so you don't forget it while you work on your chorus.

Chorus – Melody Tips

There are a lot of different melody patterns for choruses. Try this suggestion or use one of the patterns in Part Four, "Start With a Melody Pattern."

- **Make Your First Line Stand Out.** Draw attention to the first line of your chorus melody with a jump up or down in pitch. Or add rhythmic interest with a repeated note or riff-like phrase.

- **Repeat a melody line.** Repeat your first melody line with different lyrics. Listeners get to hear a strong melody again and new lyrics keep it interesting.

- **Vary your phrase lengths.** A series of phrases that are all the same length can start to feel predictable. Try a couple of short, repeated melodic phrases in the middle of your chorus, or lengthen a line and run it into the next one to create an extra long phrase.

- **Give your final line added weight.** The last line of the chorus — the payoff line — should be strong and memorable, something listeners can recall long after the song is over. Give the melody a twist or add a pause to make listeners notice it. You can repeat the end of the melody phrase or create extra length be adding words and notes to make this line say, "Listen to me!"

- **Use contrast.** Make your whole chorus stand out by putting it in a different note range than the verse — higher or lower — or changing the pace of the notes and words — more notes per beat or fewer, longer notes.

> **HOT TIP:** _**Use a hit song melody pattern.**_ If you're having trouble coming up with a melody, listen to a few successful songs you like and notice which melody lines are repeated, whether there's a variety of long and short phrases, and where the melody adds rhythmic interest. Try something similar in your own song.

STAGE 2: CHORDS

- **Make your chords and melody work together.** Make sure your chords are supporting the melodies of verse and chorus. Although emphasizing a note that's not in the accompanying chord can add complexity and depth to your melody, if you're singing a melody note that's _fighting_ a chord, consider moving it up or down or changing the chord. A very sour or dissonant note will draw attention to itself, so unless you're doing it for a reason, consider making a change.

- **Adjust the chords.** When using a very repetitive three- or four-chord progression, consider creating some variety when you get to the chorus by adding an extra note to one of the chords (the 2nd or 4th) or changing a bass note. Or you can substitute one chord for another, similar chord.

Record your STAGE 2 draft

In this recording, try to get a feel for the rise and fall of energy between verse and chorus. Use a metronome click or rhythm track to keep the tempo steady. If you haven't already chosen a drum or percussion groove to write to, check out Part Three, "Start With a Rhythm Track," for resources.

Record your first verse and chorus — lyrics, melody, and chords. You haven't written lyrics for your second verse yet, so just play the chords and hum the melody during Verse 2. Don't aim for perfection. At this stage, you're just trying to capture a sense of flow. When you finish recording, take a break.

THE THIRD STAGE

LISTEN AND MAKE CHANGES

Play the recording of your second draft. Imagine you're hearing your verse and chorus for the first time, like a new listener will. This is the time to check out the relationship between your song's verse and chorus. A verse lyric should lead to and set up the chorus lyric. The chorus melody should feel like it raises the energy level of the song. There should be enough contrast between the verse and chorus for listeners to know when the song moves from one section to the other.

- **STEP 1) Make a "to do" list.** Write down any ideas you have or changes you want to make as the song plays. Work through the items on your list. If you like your changes, keep them. If you don't, go back to what you had.

- **STEP 2) Adjust the fit of lyrics and melody.** If you find that you're crowding too many words into a short space or your lyric is causing awkward rhythms in the melody, do a little lyric rewriting. It's often easy to drop out a word or two without changing the meaning of a line. On the other hand, if you're writing a quirky song with some intentionally awkward moments, be sure those are handled consistently so it's clear you meant to do it.

STAGE 3: FILL IN THE SONG STRUCTURE

Now you're ready to complete your song structure with lyrics for Verse 2, a Bridge section, a final Chorus, an intro and an ending.

Verse 2 – Lyric Tips

- **Answer the questions.** Look at the lyrics you've written for Verse 1 and the chorus, and then decide what you still need to tell your listeners so they can understand what the singer is feeling. Here are some things you could write about in your second verse: What led up to this moment? What does the singer hope (or is afraid) will happen next? What has been lost or found? Why is this important to the singer? If the singer is talking to or about someone else, show the listener what the singer sees in that other person.

- **Add life to your lyric.** Bring your lyric to life with actions and dialogue. ("When you stumbled into my life…" "When you said you loved me and I said…"). Use physical sensations to make listeners feel what the singer is feeling ("the cold, sharp ice in your eyes" "the thunder of my heart").

Verse 2 – Melody Tip

The vocal melody of the second verse will generally be the same as the first verse, with adjustments for different lyrics.

STAGE 3: ADD A VOCAL BRIDGE

Many of today's successful songs have a vocal bridge after the second chorus. Two to four lines will do it, longer if you feel like it.

Bridge – Lyric Tip

- **Try an insight or reveal.** The bridge lyric adds something the listener hasn't heard before — for example, something the singer has learned from this experience, or the singer's most intimate thoughts, hopes, or fears.

Bridge – Melody Tips

- **Create melodic contrast.** Make it clear your bridge is a whole new section of the song by changing up the melody. Try something different from both the chorus and the verse. Use shorter or longer line lengths, vary the pace and note range in the bridge melody.

- **Vary the chord progression.** You can create contrast with chords, too. Try adding related chords you haven't used previously or changing the chords at a different rate. You can even stay on a single chord throughout the bridge. Explore a few different ideas until you find something you like.

STAGE 3: ADD THE FINAL CHORUS, OUTRO, AND INTRO

- **Return and wrap up.** After the bridge you can return to your chorus or to a pre-chorus if you have one. Depending on the length of your song and how much repetition you want, you can sing your entire chorus twice or sing it once and repeat the final lines of the chorus. This is called a "tag."

- **Button ending or fade out.** Decide if you want your song to fade out electronically or have a definitive ending — a chord or note than rings out naturally. For the Film & TV market, a definitive or "button" ending is preferred. This means that the song arrives at a final note or chord that is allowed to ring out naturally. Currently, many radio hits feature this type of natural ending, rather than a fade out created by the engineer while the music continues to play. There's no right or wrong way to end your track. It's a matter of taste and what feels right for the song.

- **Keep your intro short.** When you finish working on the end of your song, take a few minutes to think about the beginning. Consider keeping your intro brief. If you're using a three- or four-chord progression, play it only once. Listeners like to get to the vocal. If you feel you need a long intro, record two versions. Pitch the shorter intro to the music industry. Use the longer one on your album.

STAGE 3: TUNE UP YOUR RHYMES

- **Focus on rhymes.** You may have some lines that ought to rhyme but don't. Others that don't look like rhymes on the page, but sound fine when you sing them. Decide which lines need a rhyming tune-up.

- **Perfect rhymes or near rhymes?** Today's rhyming style is loose and relaxed. Perfect rhymes can sound too predictable, so try "near rhymes" or "vowel rhymes" — words that have the same vowel sound but different consonants. A rhyming dictionary can be helpful if it includes near rhymes. Here are some online rhyming resources: B-rhymes.com, WikiRhymer.com, Rhymedesk.com (At Rhymedesk, type in the word you want to rhyme. Choose "Near Rhymes." Look under "Assonances" for vowel rhymes.)

Record your STAGE 3 draft

Make a rough recording of your song from top to bottom. Try to capture the feel you want the final song to have. Be sure to record to a steady metronome click or the rhythm track you've been working with. Once you've roughed out a complete recording, you'll have a good idea how long your song will run.

- **Check the length.** Take a look at the overall length of your song. Some hit songs are longer than four minutes but not many. Most music publishers recommend a length of around 3:30, with the first chorus occurring one minute or less into the song.

- **To shorten your song.** Use a single chorus at the end and a short tag. Eliminate extra bars of instrumental between verses and choruses and cut down the length of your intro. Be a tough critic: Do you really need that double verse in the beginning? Can you shorten the length of the verse or pre-chorus?

- **To lengthen your song.** If your song is two minutes or less, you can add a bridge section. Double the length of your first verse or add a pre-chorus between each verse and chorus. Or try a double chorus at the end of the song.

> **_HOT TIP: Write for the Film & TV song market._** Songs that are longer than four minutes or as short as two and a half minutes are not a problem for this market. Listen to successful film and TV songs to get a feel for the lengths that works best.

After recording, take a break and come back later to work on your final draft.

THE FOURTH STAGE

Listen to the rough recording of your third draft with fresh ears. Do you feel it expresses what you want to say? Does it convey the emotion you want your listeners to feel? Does the chorus seem memorable? Write down any changes you want to make. Go through your list and rewrite as needed. As always, if you like a change, keep it. If you don't, go back to what you had and try something different.

STAGE 4: CHECKLIST

- **Check for clearly defined song sections.** If you haven't already done so, make sure you have plenty of contrast between your verse and chorus melodies. You can raise the chorus to a higher note range or just add a high harmony part to lift it. You can change the pace of the words and notes between sections — for example, a busy verse melody versus a smooth chorus. Change phrase lengths. Try short lines in the verse and long phrases in the chorus or vice versa. A clear change from one song section to the next creates a sense of structure, something that appeals to listeners. They tend to avoid songs that wander, are formless, or are too repetitive.

- **Check your melody patterns.** The mix of repetition and variation is what makes a melody memorable and keeps it interesting. Too much repetition can become boring; too much variation can make a melody sound aimless. You want a balance of the two. Listen to your favorite successful songs and look for the patterns of repetition and variation in the melody, then check to see how your melody compares. In this book, the section titled "Start with a Melody Pattern" includes many patterns you can use.

- **Check your key lines.** The "key lines" are the first and last lines of your chorus and the first lyric line of each verse. These are the lines that listeners are most likely to hear and remember. Make each of these lyric lines something that will draw listeners in and make them want to know more. Give your melody an extra edge on these lines, too. Check to see if you could add some rhythmic syncopation, a pause, or a jump in pitch to grab attention.

- **Pump up your lyrics.** Go through your lyrics to check for weak lines or lines that sound like they belong in a different song. Replace these with something from your raw material list, or add images, comparisons, and examples directly into your lyric. Don't throw anything away until you come up with something you like better.

- **Answer the questions listeners might have.** Sometimes a lyric brings up more questions than it answers. If you referred to something outside of the song, something that happened in the past, or a conversation that the listener doesn't know about, you can either delete that reference or rewrite the lyric to tie it into the song.

- **Tighten the lyric focus.** Make sure that every line is related to the emotional message of your song. All the lines in your song should lead to and support your core idea, the one you wrote down when you started your first draft. And remember, sometimes a simple, direct statement is the most effective way to tell your listeners what you want them to know.

Record your STAGE 4 draft

Record your final draft and take a break. Come back and listen with fresh ears. If you hear anything you want to change, go ahead and do it now. If the changes are substantial, record another draft, take a break, and listen again. Do this until you're satisfied.

These "tweak" drafts are important because they give your song a final polish and ensure that you won't have any regrets later on. When you're satisfied that your song is the way you want it, it's time to put this puppy to bed.

If you're going to pitch your song to a record label, music publisher, producer, or artist, be sure the rhythm track, chords, melody, and lyric are working together to create the energy and impact that a final, commercial production will have. The vocal is especially important; it needs to put the emotion of the song across to everyone who hears it. Your demo arrangement doesn't need to have all the bells and whistles of a commercial production, but the *feel* of the final radio production needs to be there.

If your final demo is simply produced and well recorded, you may be able to pitch a bare-bones demo to the Film & TV market. An expressive piano/vocal or guitar/vocal recording can work beautifully under an emotional scene in a TV drama.

Meanwhile, use your recording to copyright your song. Visit the U.S. copyright office online at www.Copyright.gov for instructions on how to do it. If you belong to a PRO, such as ASCAP or BMI, register your song. Then upload a simple lyric video to YouTube and share it with friends and fans. Congratulate yourself and enjoy the applause. You've earned it!

PART EIGHT

REFERENCE TRACKS: THE SONGWRITER'S PROBLEM SOLVER

I don't usually pick up a software manual until I need to solve a really big problem. By then, of course, I'm frustrated. I'm yelling at the code monkeys who moved stuff around for no reason in my newly upgraded software and I'm ready to toss the whole thing in the garbage. The Troubleshooting page is no help because it says things like "Be sure your equipment is plugged in," which has never yet been the cause of my problem. The manual is 800 pages long, and there's no way to know even where to start looking because I don't know what they call the thing I need to know about.

But... I'd like to share with you the one troubleshooting resource, the one "equipment manual" I've found that seriously *works* for songwriters. It's called "reference tracks." There are about a gazillion uses for reference tracks in all styles and at all levels of songwriting. And these wonderfully useful little problem solvers are readily available. They're right there on the radio, on your laptop, your iPod, tablet, and smartphone. All you need to do is listen, really listen. Drill down into the writing, performance, arranging, and mixing to learn what you need to know to write and record competitive material.

Studying and using a reference track doesn't mean you'll end up sounding like that track any more than reading an equipment manual will make you sound like anyone else who reads that manual. Reference tracks are tools. Use them as templates, teachers, and inspiration to bring your own ideas to life.

SONGWRITING REFERENCE TRACKS

To use a reference track to help you with lyric writing, melody, or chords, start by finding successful songs you like in a genre you want to write in. If a song makes you say, "I wish I'd written that!" then it's probably a good songwriting reference track. Look through the Billboard Top Hits of the last few years. Listen to the current crop of hits on the Billboard charts. You can also find music charts at BDSradio.com. Or use your own CD library or iTunes playlists.

CHORD PROGRESSIONS

LEARN NEW CHORD PROGRESSIONS. Many of today's biggest hits are based on familiar three- and four-chord progressions that are not copyrighted, like the ones on the list below and in Part Two, "Song Starters: Chords." You can use reference tracks to help you find and learn how to use simple, repetitive progressions like these.

Remember, you must avoid using any of the instrumental arrangement, riffs, or hooks used in the hit song. Only the chords. Write them out and play them in your own style, with your own rhythm groove. If you still feel you're too close to the reference song, change some of the chords.

ACQUIRE NEW CHORD & MELODY SKILLS. Get a feel for the way today's melodies relate to these repetitive chord progressions. Learn to sing and play a hit like "Highway Don't Care" (Tim McGraw), "All of Me" (John Legend), or any of the songs listed in the Chord Starters section of this book. Notice where the chords change versus where the melody phrases start. Often these happen in two different places. If you tend to start your melody phrases in step with the chord changes, break that habit. Get comfortable with this technique by playing along with reference songs.

SONG STRUCTURE

FIND A STRUCTURE TEMPLATE. You can use a reference song to suggest the structural form of a new song. Identify the broad structure of a reference song — verses, chorus, and bridge. Make a note of each section in the order it appears in the song. Use this basic structure as a template. Just write your verse where the verses are in the reference song, your chorus where theirs is, and so on.

MAKE USE OF STRUCTURE DETAILS. In addition to the broad outline, you can follow the structure of the reference song in more detail. Does the reference song have a pre-chorus — a short section between the verse and chorus? Does it have a catchy repeated vocal or instrumental hook at the end of the chorus — called a "post-chorus"? If so, try one in your own song. How long is the intro? Make yours the same length. What happens at the end of the song? Is the whole chorus repeated or just part of it? Does it fade out or have a definitive (button) ending? You do the same.

COPY SECTION LENGTH: If you're wondering how long to make your verse or chorus, make them around the same length as the reference song.

PICK UP CONTRAST & TRANSITION IDEAS: How did you know when the reference song moved from verse to chorus? Often a change in the note range or pace of the melody will make it obvious. Try something similar in one of your own songs. How did the reference song transition from verse to chorus? Was it abrupt? Was there an unusual chord or melody changeup? And how did it move from the end of the chorus to the beginning of the next section? Try those transition ideas in a song of your own and see what happens.

LYRICS

TURN ON THE CREATIVITY SWITCH. Sometimes it's hard to get in the lyric-writing mood. You want to work on something, but no really good lines are coming, not even any "not-half-bad" lines. Now's the time to turn to your reference tracks. Spend a few minutes listening to the lyrics in successful songs you like. Pay attention to the way they describe emotion in images and actions, how they use a word you didn't expect. Write a few lines that might work in one of their songs. Then write a few more. Turn off the music and keep writing.

GET IDEAS FOR OPENING LINES. Can't think of a good opening line? Again, take a look at the lyrics to a few successful songs in your genre. How did they grab attention right at the start? How did they drop you into the middle of the action? Did they use a strong statement, a question, or a line of dialogue? All of these will get listeners involved. Or did your reference songs come up with a different way to do it? Try *that!*

FIND TIPS ON FOCUS AND DEVELOPMENT. Second verses can be tricky. And the bridge! What *will* you say in your bridge? If you can't think of anything to say next, go listen to a few of your favorite songs to see how they solved that problem. Write a one-line summary of the information in the first verse and chorus. How did the second verse build on that? Did it describe the singer's feelings in more depth? Paint a picture of the other person involved? Or talk about what the singer planned to do next? What did the bridge reveal that we didn't already know? Try that in your own song.

TO BE POETIC OR NOT TO BE. You know what you want to say, but you're not sure how to get it across to listeners. Should you be poetic and evocative, or is it better to simply say it straight out? Often a combination of the two works well, but how much of each should you use? Time to check those reference songs. Choose songs with lyrics you like and admire. Take a look at the mix of imagery and poetic comparisons versus direct statements about what's happening. Then go back to your lyric and see if you want to add more of one or the other. It's up to you, of course. Just be sure you don't leave your listeners wondering what's going on in your song.

USE REFERENCE SONGS AS "GHOST SONGS." In my books, I talk about using hit songs as "ghost songs." If you're a lyricist, consider writing your lyric to the melody of a recent hit song. It will help you avoid falling into predictable "greeting card" patterns. Once you have a verse and chorus lyric, hand it off to a co-writer. Don't tell your collaborator about the "ghost" song. Let them come up with a brand new melody, and then finish your lyric using the new melody.

MELODY

GET IN A MELODY MOOD. You can use reference songs to rev up your creativity for melody writing. Play a few successful songs you like. As you listen, notice the points at which a good melody lifts the energy and drops it back down, defines the structure of the song, and creates an expectation and then breaks it. ("Hey, I thought they were going to do that again but they didn't!") You can also pick up ideas for rhythmic feel and grooves while you listen. Hum or play along with a song. Then turn off the music and keep going on your own.

GET IDEAS FOR USING REPETITION AND VARIATION. If you don't have enough repetition, your melody will be hard to remember. If you have too much it will become predictable. So, how much melodic repetition is too much? Listen to the melodies of successful songs in the style you want to write in and make a note of the number of times a melody line is repeated in a song section (with or without the same lyric) and where it changes to something new. Note how often the new melody repeats and whether it returns to the first idea again. Try using that pattern in a song of your own.

LEARN HOW TO CREATE FORWARD MOMENTUM. Irresistible forward momentum is a hallmark of today's big hit song melodies. Listen to almost any current Pop, Rock, or Country hit and you'll hear a verse melody that starts out at a conversational pace, with plenty of breathing space, then takes off like a rocket in the chorus. By eliminating pauses between lines in the chorus melody, the songwriter can create a feeling of momentum. Notice how the songwriters run one line into the next, sometimes adding short pauses in places where you don't expect. Sing along with one of these big hits, and then try this technique in a verse and chorus melody of your own.

PERFORMANCE REFERENCE TRACKS

LEARN VOCAL PHRASING. When you listen to successful singer-songwriters like John Mayer, Joshua Radin, Ingrid Michaelson, and Jack Johnson, you might notice that these artists almost never raise their voices above a conversational level. They don't use big changes in volume. They would never win a TV voice competition. What are they doing that makes their vocals so appealing? Sing along with some of these artists' recordings to get a feel for the phrasing and rhythm of their performances. Try to match their phrase starts, note attacks, and releases. If a singer breaks from chest into head voice, you try that. Notice how the singer relates to the underlying beat. Are they laying back then catching up? Or staying on top of the beat? How much rhythm is in their vocal performances?

What if you don't have the Pop pipes of a Kelly Clarkson or the Rock rasp of a David Grohl? You can learn some of their phrasing techniques by listening to their hits. Then blend those with your own style to come up with something new. Or book a session with a vocal coach and take your reference tracks along. Ask the coach to show you how some specific things are done.

You're not doing this in order to imitate these singers. You're looking for techniques you can use to express emotion and character in your own songs. Once you have these techniques under your belt, you'll be able to choose the right one at the right time, the one that tells listeners what you honestly feel when you sing your lyric.

EXPAND YOUR INSTRUMENT SOUNDS. Most guitar players have spent hours listening to recordings, learning guitar solos, riffs, and strums. So, for you guitar players, reference tracks should be pretty familiar. Keep up to date by studying the guitar tracks on recent hits. Today's electric guitar sounds are different from those that were popular in the '70s and '80s. Unless you're intentionally blending current and retro, you'll want to update your electric guitar settings. The same goes for keyboard players. Study recent hits or pick up a retro vibe from vintage styles to blend with contemporary elements.

LEARN TODAY'S ARRANGEMENT STYLES. With the accessibility of home recording studios, songwriters are often playing not only basic guitar tracks, but also keyboard, drums, synthesizer, and even entire orchestral arrangements. Listen to reference tracks in the style you're working in to get creative ideas for building and developing your arrangements, both the instruments to use and the way their played.

CHECK YOUR INSTRUMENTAL PERFORMANCE. How confident, clean, and tight does an acoustic rhythm guitar or keyboard performance need to be? The answer: It needs to be as confident, clean, and tight as the performances on the recordings you'll be competing with in your genre and market. In all mainstream genres, the level of playing adds energy and supports the emotional feel of the song. Unless you're aiming for a lo-fi vibe, a wobbly or out-of-tune performance will be a distraction for listeners. Keep a list of recordings with guitar, keyboard, and drum performances you want to emulate and use them as a reference when you record your tracks.

PRODUCER REFERENCE TRACKS

SHOW YOUR PRODUCER WHAT YOU WANT. If you're hiring a music producer to produce your song, playing reference tracks for each other is *essential*. There's no better way to describe music than playing music. If you have a genre in mind, a certain instrumental arrangement sound, a rhythm groove, or guitar sound you want, play an example for the producer. You might play several reference tracks, one with a drum sound you like, another with a vocal sound, etc.

DISCUSS IDEAS WITH YOUR PRODUCER. Have the producer play reference tracks for you, too. How does he or she hear your sound? What general style are they going to aim for? You're not going to end up with exactly the same sound, but you'll *both* have an idea which direction the song is headed… the *same* idea. If the arrangement veers off too much, go back and play the reference tracks for each other again. It will save time and money and help you get what you want.

MIXING REFERENCE TRACKS

KEEP YOUR MIX ON TRACK. You've been mixing that happy, upbeat track for ten hours now and it's starting to sound dark and ominous instead of quirky and fun. So you brighten it up with a little EQ. Then you brighten it up some more, and a little more. Pretty soon it's so piercing, only the neighborhood dogs can hear it. Stop. Listen to a reference track in the style you want. Let it remind your ears of what you started out to do. Adjust the EQ and move on.

LEARN FROM PRO MIXES. Reference tracks won't teach you how to use your equipment, at least not at first. But there are mentors, classes, books, and online courses that can give you the knob-twiddling basics. Then turn to your reference tracks. Choose a sound you want to work on — deep background pads, Marshall-stack electric guitar, or dry, punchy drums — and try to recreate it on your own equipment. Get as close as you can. Save your settings and pull them up next time you need that sound.

REFERENCE TRACKS FOR SONG PITCHING

Song pitching is one of the most widespread uses of reference tracks. Everybody in the music business uses reference tracks to describe: A) the type of music, artist, or song they are looking for, or B) the type of music, artist or song they are offering. If you're a songwriter or performer, you're in category B.

TELL THEM WHO YOU ARE SPEEDILY. Let's say you get a phone call from an A&R exec, a major music publisher, or a Grammy-winning producer and they say: "I hear you write songs. What kind of songs do you write?" If you say "good songs," they will get busy on another phone call right away. They need a quick, clear idea of your genre, sound, and the market your songs are aimed at. So a better answer would be two or three reference artists: "My music is similar to Beach House, Tame Impala, and Cage the Elephant." Or you might say, "My songs are in the style of Katy Perry, Kelly Clarkson, and OneRepublic." Each set of references tells the music industry person the genre, the market, and something about the sound of your music. It doesn't tell them how good you are. But if they work in one of those markets (the College market or Mainstream Pop radio), they will probably ask to hear your music.

PLAYLISTS: ORGANIZE YOUR REFERENCE TRACKS

There are times when you hear a song and think, "What a cool piano sound! I want a piano sound like that in one of my songs." So, how do you find that song again when you need it? Add that song to a *playlist* called "Instrument sounds – Piano."

A playlist can be as simple as a file on your laptop or smartphone. If you have a database program like Excel, use that. Make a note of the song title and a brief description of what you like in the song. Is it the instrumental arrangement or mix? Is it the lyrics or melody? If it's more than one thing, enter the song in several places.

There's no right or wrong way to organize your playlists. Whatever works best for you is the way to do it. Make a note of any track that you think might come in handy as a reference and add a short description.

WHERE DO YOU FIND GOOD REFERENCE TRACKS?

You've already got a good start on your reference tracks — the artists and songs you have in your own music collection. Go through them periodically and look for tracks that might be useful. Add them to your playlists where you can find them.

If you create your playlists in iTunes, Spotify, or Apple Music, then make several, one for each type of reference track (lyrics, melody, arrangement, vocal performance, mix, artist style). use the comment section to add descriptive tags so you can search for "dark piano sound," "dry drums," "70s vibe," "lyric images," or "good Country vocal."

Every track should be there for a reason, one that you've made a note of so you can find it when you need it. If you do that, your reference tracks will quickly become one of your most useful resources, and one you'll come back to again and again.

» KEEP WRITING AND NEVER STOP

Now that you've reached the end of this book, you've probably realized, as I have, that there's an endless supply of words, melodies, harmonies, characters, insights, memories, and stories to feed our creative energy. This source of artistic nourishment is all around us every day, in the people we know, the entertainment we watch, the lives we lead.

Expressing thoughts and feelings in song is something humans have felt compelled to do for millennia and we still haven't run out of things to say. Nevertheless, we sometimes find ourselves stuck and we need a little push.

ADD SONGWRITING SESSIONS TO YOUR BUSY LIFE

Songwriting doesn't have to wait until you have three or four hours of guaranteed quiet time stretching out before you. I mean, who has that anyway? If you're having trouble finding time to write, try working in short, intense bursts. Give yourself a time limit: 45 minutes or less. Take it seriously. Time yourself and stop when your time is up.

There are plenty of advantages to working this way.

- You'll maintain better focus on your work. No snacking, wandering around, or cruising the internet.

- Short writing sessions prevent burnout, overthinking, or losing perspective on your song.

- If you stop while you still have things you want to work on, you'll look forward to starting your next writing session, which means you'll find time to do it.

Try it now. Use one of the Song Starters in this book, set a timer for 45 minutes, and do as much as you can. When the timer goes off, stop. Be sure to write out your lyric or make a rough recording during the last few minutes of your session. Tomorrow, play your recording or read your lyric, make a list of things you'd like to do, and go to work.

FIND CO-WRITERS, SUPPORTERS, AND FRIENDS

Songwriting can be a solitary gig sometimes. While it's good to draw on inner resources, there are times when you need to replenish those resources with input from the outside world. A co-writer can bring new skills to a project and encourage you to complete drafts, keeping the process moving along. Meeting with other songwriters to share works-in-progress can be a great way to get feedback and help when you've got a problem to solve. Sometimes it's just a good idea to hang out with people who go through the same ups and downs that you do.

If there's a college or learning extension program in your area, take a class in songwriting, singing, guitar, or piano playing. You're likely to meet a few songwriters there. Continue to meet after the class is over to share new songs. Check out open mic nights at local clubs. When you hear a band or artist you like, ask if they're interested in meeting to talk about writing together or being part of your songwriting group.

PRACTICE YOUR SONGWRITING SKILLS

If you've ever taken piano lessons, you probably remember your teacher urging you to "Practice. Practice. Practice." And when you did practice, you became a better player. Songwriting is the same: The more you practice, the more confident, faster, and better you get. Keep using and re-using the Song Starters to help you work up new material. Then, follow the suggestions in "Write a Song in Four Stages" to develop your ideas into complete songs.

GIVE YOURSELF A ROUND OF APPLAUSE... OR TWO OR THREE OR FOUR.

People who are not songwriters think what we do is easy. But we know better. Yes, it can be exciting, joyful, enriching, and surprising. It can also be slogging hard work. But the songs at the end of all the madness are worth it. So, give yourself kudos, bravos, congratulations, pats on the back, and a standing ovation or two. Do it often and with great enthusiasm. You deserve it for undertaking the challenge of simply starting a song. You don't ever need to say, "I want to be a songwriter." Instead, say: "I *am* a songwriter."

May your songs flow.

» LEARN MORE: SONGWRITERS TELL ALL

Songwriters love to talk about songwriting. Here's a list of successful songwriters who have discussed the craft of songwriting and their own songwriting process in interviews, books, and articles. An internet search for a songwriter's name plus "songwriting interview" or "songwriting podcast" will turn up plenty of gold. Take a look at an autobiography like Jimmy Webb's *Tunesmith* for useful insights into his store knowledge and experience. Books about bands and artists, like Ian MacDonald's *Revolution In The Head,* detailing the writing and recording of every Beatles' song, can offer valuable insights into the songwriting process as well.

Discover where successful songwriters find their inspiration. Research how they get their songs started and developed, how they collaborate and rewrite. Then try these ideas yourself. Adapt or blend them with your own writing process. Keep what works. Throw out what doesn't. Continue looking, listening, reading, and absorbing new ideas. There's always something new to try.

Adele
Alanis Morissette
Alicia Keys
Ashley Gorley
Barry Mann and Cynthia Weill
Billy Joel
Bob Dylan
Bono
Brian Wilson
Bruce Springsteen
Burt Bacharach and Hal David
Carole King
David Bowie
Diane Warren

Ed Sheeran
Elton John
Elvis Costello
Holland, Dozier, Holland
Jackson Browne
Jason Mraz
Jay-Z
Jimmy Webb
John Legend
John Lennon
Joni Mitchell
Kendrick Lamar
Leonard Cohen
Lucinda Williams
Mark Knopfler
Neil Young
Paul McCartney
Paul Simon
Randy Newman
Ray Wylie Hubbard
Rosanne Cash
Ross Copperman
Ryan Tedder
Sia Furler
Smokey Robinson
Stephen Sondheim
Stevie Nicks
Stevie Wonder
Sting
Tom Kelly & Billy Steinberg
Willie Nelson

» INDEX

» SONG INDEX

» ABOUT THE AUTHOR

Robin Frederick is the author of popular songwriting books *Shortcuts to Hit Songwriting, Shortcuts to Songwriting for Film & TV, Study the Hits,* and *The 30-Minute Songwriter.* She's a former Director of A&R for Rhino Records, executive producer of more than 60 albums, and an in-demand lecturer in the music industry. She has written and produced hundreds of songs for television, records, theater, and audio products. A former Vice President of the Los Angeles Chapter of the Recording Academy (the Grammy organization) and former President of Los Angeles Women in Music, Robin is currently active in numerous music industry organizations.

To sign up for Robin's Songwriting Tips newsletter, visit her website at RobinFrederick.com.

» BOOK REVIEWS

Robin's books are available at Amazon.com and other retail book outlets. Here's what the music industry is saying:

SHORTCUTS TO HIT SONGWRITING

"Great reference material for people serious about writing great songs. It's got it all!"

KARA DIOGUARDI – *BMI "Songwriter of the Year," Grammy-nominated hit songwriter with sales of more than 100 million records.*

"This book is truly what its title proclaims–126 concrete tools to kick start your songwriting or take it to the next level. Written in an easy-to-understand, accessible style, *Shortcuts to Hit Songwriting* should be in every songwriter's arsenal."

JASON BLUME – *Hit songwriter with more than 50 million album sales, songwriting teacher, and author of 6 Steps to Songwriting Success.*

"An excellent road map for writers at all levels. When you set out for success, it's so easy to slip off the path–this is the songwriter's GPS!"

RALPH MURPHY – *Vice President, ASCAP Nashville*

"This is a superbly written and organized Swiss Army knife of a songwriting manual with 126 sharp tools, tips, exercises, and insights for every stage of creating your songs. Whether you want to write hits or just the most powerful expressions of your concepts, feelings, or stories, you'll find this toolbox an easy-to-read, fun, and indispensable teacher."

JOHN BRAHENY – *Author of "The Craft and Business of Songwriting"*

SHORTCUTS TO SONGWRITING FOR FILM & TV

"This book is worth its weight in gold! It will save you a lot of time, heartache, and could make you a lot of money!"

JIM LONG – *Legendary music library pioneer and innovator; Firstcom, OneMusic, and Crucial Music*

"Truly a great resource for anyone who wants to get their music used in Film & TV. This book is a Must-Have!"

STEPHAN R. GOLDMAN – *Music supervisor for 65 feature films, including Academy Award winners and nominees.*

"This is not merely a 'How To' book but, more importantly, a 'What Not To Do' book. It gives songwriters the edge they need to compete at a whole different level."

PETER GRECO – *17 years as Sr. Vice President of Music, Young & Rubicam, NY*

"An indispensable guide with tips for any songwriter in any genre looking to expose their future hits in Film and TV."

JAY FRANK – *Author of FutureHit.DNA,*
founder of DigSin digital record label.

Made in the USA
San Bernardino, CA
22 June 2019